The Indian Ocean in World History

The New
Oxford
World
History

The Indian
Ocean in
World History

Edward A. Alpers

OXFORD
UNIVERSITY PRESS

OXFORD

UNIVERSITY PRESS

Oxford University Press is a department of the University of Oxford.
It furthers the University's objective of excellence in research,
scholarship, and education by publishing worldwide.

Oxford   New York
Auckland   Cape Town   Dar es Salaam   Hong Kong   Karachi
Kuala Lumpur   Madrid   Melbourne   Mexico City   Nairobi
New Delhi   Shanghai   Taipei   Toronto

With offices in
Argentina   Austria   Brazil   Chile   Czech Republic   France   Greece
Guatemala   Hungary   Italy   Japan   Poland   Portugal   Singapore
South Korea   Switzerland   Thailand   Turkey   Ukraine   Vietnam

Oxford is a registered trade mark of Oxford University Press
in the UK and certain other countries.

Published in the United States of America by
Oxford University Press
198 Madison Avenue, New York, NY 10016

Library of Congress Cataloging-in-Publication Data
Alpers, Edward A.
The Indian Ocean in world history / Edward A. Alpers.
pages cm.—(New Oxford world history)
Includes bibliographical references and index.
ISBN 978-0-19-533787-7 (alk. paper)—ISBN 978-0-19-516593-7 (alk. paper)
1. Indian Ocean Region–Civilization. 2. Indian Ocean Region–History. I. Title.
DS340.A47   2013
909′.09824—dc23   2013020136

Frontispiece: Eruption of the Krakatoa volcano, 1883. Royal Society Report on
Krakatoa Eruption (Parker & Coward, 1888)

For my brother, Paul J. Alpers (1932–2013)

Contents

Editors' Preface

This book is part of the New Oxford World History, an innovative series that offers readers an informed, lively, and up-to-date history of the world and its people that represents a significant change from the "old" world history. Only a few years ago, world history generally amounted to a history of the West—Europe and the United States—with small amounts of information from the rest of the world. Some versions of the "old" world history drew attention to every part of the world *except* Europe and the United States. Readers of that kind of world history could get the impression that somehow the rest of the world was made up of exotic people who had strange customs and spoke difficult languages. Still another kind of "old" world history presented the story of areas or peoples of the world by focusing primarily on the achievements of great civilizations. One learned of great buildings, influential world religions, and mighty rulers but little of ordinary people or more general economic and social patterns. Interactions among the world's peoples were often told from only one perspective.

This series tells world history differently. First, it is comprehensive, covering all countries and regions of the world and investigating the total human experience—even those of so-called peoples without histories living far from the great civilizations. "New" world historians thus share in common an interest in all of human history, even going back millions of years before there were written human records. A few "new" world histories even extend their focus to the entire universe, a "big history" perspective that dramatically shifts the beginning of the story back to the big bang. Some see the "new" global framework of world history today as viewing the world from the vantage point of the Moon, as one scholar put it. We agree. But we also want to take a close-up view, analyzing and reconstructing the significant experiences of all of humanity.

This is not to say that everything that has happened everywhere and in all time periods can be recovered or is worth knowing, but that there is much to be gained by considering both the separate and interrelated stories of different societies and cultures. Making these connections is still another crucial ingredient of the "new" world history. It emphasizes connectedness and interactions of all kinds—cultural, economic, political, religious, and social—involving peoples, places, and processes. It makes comparisons and finds similarities. Emphasizing both the comparisons and interactions is critical to developing a global framework that can deepen and broaden historical understanding, whether the focus is on a specific country or region or on the whole world.

The rise of the new world history as a discipline comes at an opportune time. The interest in world history in schools and among the general public is vast. We travel to one another's nations, converse and work with people around the world, and are changed by global events. War and peace affect populations worldwide as do economic conditions and the state of our environment, communications, and health and medicine. The New Oxford World History presents local histories in a global context and gives an overview of world events seen through the eyes of ordinary people. This combination of the local and the global further defines the new world history. Understanding the workings of global and local conditions in the past gives us tools for examining our own world and for envisioning the interconnected future that is in the making.

Bonnie G. Smith
Anand Yang

CHAPTER I

Imagining the Indian Ocean

For many years the Indian Ocean was the least studied of the world's great oceanic systems. This situation is now changing. Historians know that there have been major economic and cultural exchanges across its waters and around its coasts that date back at least seven thousand years and that these were greatly accelerated following the rise and expansion of Islam from the seventh century CE. Among the many challenges to understanding the dynamics of this important world region is how best to define it, for unlike continental land masses oceanic boundaries are, literally, more fluid. One way to approach this problem is to read what various travelers have written about sailing its waters.

"It was the first week in December when we sailed from Aden, and the northeast monsoon was blowing very quietly." Thus writes sailor-adventurer Alan Villiers as he began his voyage from Kuwait aboard the *Triumph of Righteousness* in 1938, headed toward the East African coast and returning around the coast of Arabia. His ship was a boom, a large type of Arab sailing vessel that plied the waters of the Indian Ocean in the twentieth century. "I knew this was the kind of vessel in which I wished to sail," he recalls. "The atmosphere of true adventure and romance lay heavy on her graceful hull, and the very timbers of her worn decks were impregnated with the spirit of colorful wandering."[1] Villiers lamented: "It seemed to me, having looked far and wide over twenty years of a seafaring life, that as pure sailing craft carrying on their unspoiled ways, only the Arab remained. Only the Arab remained making his voyages as he always had, in a wind-driven vessel sailing without the benefit of engines. Only the Arab still sailed his wind ships over the free sea, keeping steadfastly to the quieter ways of a kinder past."[2]

Two decades later, in the 1950s, early in the Southwest Monsoon, American journalist William M. Holden sailed the return journey from

Zanzibar to Oman on board the Indian dhow *Harisagar*. Although a landlubber, Holden's first impressions of sailing the ocean echo those of the experienced sailor Villiers. "I lay awake for hours, listening to the sounds of the ship versus wind and sea, and the snoring sounds of our passage. Just as sailing ships have from times earlier than written records, *Harisagar* was adventuring far out onto the primeval sea—sail swollen with wind, teak deck heaving, timbers creaking. Spindrift touched flesh like cool fingertips. We would sail thousands of miles across the Indian deep, through whatever caprices of monsoon weather lay in store."[3]

Although both Villiers and Holden wrote in the twentieth century, their sentimental observations recapture a pattern of maritime trade that marks the entire history of the Indian Ocean. Traders exchanged goods, and sailors manned the boats that carried those goods along the coasts of the northwest Indian Ocean long before the rise of Islam in the seventh century CE and the kind of seafaring the passing of which Villiers regrets. From the Harappa civilization of the Indus Valley (c. 2600–1900 BCE), coasting vessels transported goods from what is today the coast of modern Pakistan to the Arab or Persian Gulf—hereafter simply the Gulf—to the Red Sea, and eventually to Egypt. Also, the Indonesian settlement of Madagascar bears witness to the reality that the entire circumference of the Indian Ocean littoral was probably being traversed as early as the first centuries CE. As early as about 100 BCE there exists archaeological evidence of trade between the Mediterranean world and that of the Indian Ocean in the form of Roman coins and amphoras (ceramic vessels for carrying wine and olive oil). By about 50 CE there is documentary evidence confirming that the Greco-Roman sailors and merchants had discovered knowledge of the monsoon winds, perhaps eight centuries after sailors within the Indian Ocean region had mastered them, which determine seasonal sailing patterns in the Indian Ocean. This document was written by an unknown Alexandrian Greek and is called the *Periplus of the Erythraen Sea*. It reveals to the reader the commercial wonders to be had beyond the waters and shores of the Red Sea, branching out to the coasts of both Africa and the Indian subcontinent.

While the *Periplus* provides invaluable insight into the workings of the Indian Ocean trading system of two thousand years ago, including goods traded, the major ports of trade, and an outline of both economic and cultural exchanges between different peoples, it does not convey what it meant to sail upon the ocean itself or to experience the cultures of the Indian Ocean. To gain a more complete sense of the Indian Ocean region, we must turn instead to other travelers to conjure up its immensity. The thirteenth-century Venetian traveler Marco Polo, for example, writing in the third person, claims for himself and his companions that "they sailed over the Indian Ocean fully eighteen months before reaching their destination. And they observed many remarkable things, which will be described in this book."[4] Even as he described the Indian Ocean, however, Polo's outlook remained Venetian and Mediterranean. By contrast, the Indian Ocean that the intrepid fourteenth-century Moroccan traveler Ibn Battuta describes in his *Travels* reveals a largely Islamic world that was outward looking, interconnected, and multiethnic. It was a world that for Ibn Battuta focused on the major entrepôts or trading port cities right around the circumference of the Indian Ocean like Aden, in modern Yemen; Mogadishu, in Somalia; Kilwa, off the coast of mainland Tanzania; Zafar, in southern Arabia on the border of modern Yemen and Oman; New Hormuz, located on a desolate island off the coast of southern Iran; Calicut, modern Kozhikode, in southwestern India; Pasai, on the northern coast of Sumatra; and Zaytun, modern Quanzhou, in southern China.

Like Villiers and Holden, both Polo and Ibn Battuta were outsiders to the Indian Ocean world. More than a century after Ibn Battuta, the learned Omani navigator Ahmad ibn Majid wrote his monumental treatise on Arab navigation in the Indian Ocean. Ibn Majid's *Fawā'id* is the most comprehensive treatment of the Indian Ocean in the premodern era, but like the *Periplus*, it is a practical manual rather than a work of imagination. Nevertheless, Ibn Majid was also a poet, and he regularly intersperses his technical advice with verses that render some idea of what it meant to embark on these waters in the late fifteenth century. He writes, "When the author has finished expounding all the more important properties of the lunar mansions, rhumbs, routes, *bāshīs*, stars and their seasons . . . he should begin to explain the signs for landfalls (*ishārāt*) and the management and the organization of the ship and its crew, for although this is not in itself scientific it is characterized by this science." Ibn Majid then concludes several paragraphs of such advice with the following verses:

If I remain with those who follow not in my steps
    It is more bitter than the dangers of a stormy sea.
Give me a ship and I will take it through danger,
    For this is better than having friends who can be insincere.
At times I will accompany it through difficulties,
    At others I will divert myself with society and late nights.

If there is no escape from society or from traveling
   Or riding [the ship] then we have surely reached our final end.
This [ship] is a wonder of God, my mount, my escort.
   In travel 'tis the house of God itself.[5]

Another Muslim writer, the anonymous early sixteenth-century author of the Indonesian text *Sanghyang Siksakandang Karesian*, describes an Indian Ocean world that is defined by the different "ways of speaking" around its shores. Among the total of fifty-five locations mentioned in the text, the author identifies the four most "distant realms"—China, southern India, Persia, and Egypt—which might be regarded as the four corners of the Indian Ocean world, at least from the perspective of insular Southeast Asia. Yet, for this learned individual, just as the *Periplus* provides no descriptions beyond the South Asian subcontinent, the Indian Ocean did not extend to eastern Africa, including even Madagascar.

A different premodern outsider who attempted to capture this elusive Indian Ocean region for his readers was Luís de Camões, a poet of the Portuguese seaborne empire in the East. Camões spent seventeen years in Goa, Macao, and Mozambique before returning home in 1570 to publish his jingoistic narrative poem, *The Lusíads*, two years later. His Indian Ocean world was still significantly Muslim, but it was now marked by bitter conflict between the Portuguese Empire and local Muslim potentates that was part military, part commercial, and part religious. Camões was not sympathetic to the peoples whom the Portuguese encountered in the Indian Ocean, but he does nicely catch the initial curiosity of the Portuguese themselves that was provoked by their intrusion into this unfamiliar world. Vasco da Gama's fleet reached Mozambique Island in January 1498. Although he initially did not intend to put in there, he changed his mind because, as Camões tells us,

On the instant from the island nearest
The main there came in close company
Several small feluccas skimming
The wide bay under their broad sails.
Our people were overjoyed and could only
Stare in excitement at this wonder.
"Who are these people?" they kept exclaiming,
"What customs? What beliefs? Who is their king?"[6]

Camões concludes this episode with lines that evoke the verses of Ibn Majid and again emphasize the enormity of attempting to gain both physical and imaginative control of this vast oceanic world.

On the sea, such storms and perils
That death, many times, seemed imminent;
On the land, such battle and intrigue
Such dire, inevitable hardships!
Where may frail humanity shelter
Briefly, in some secure port,
Where the bright heavens cease to vent their rage
On such insects on so small a stage?[7]

Whether they were insiders or outsiders, each of these early writers struggled with the challenge of conveying the vastness and complexity of the Indian Ocean world. This was inevitable, considering the many different societies that were a part of the region's history. More significant, each cannot escape the ties that bind him to the place from which he viewed the Indian Ocean world.

When historians attempt to define the Indian Ocean for modern readers, they need to realize that it is not simply a substitute for a continental land mass that possesses clearly identifiable boundaries. Nor is it likely to be dominated by the political states or nations that have come to occupy center stage in the writing of most modern histories. In fact, one of the challenges of studying the history of any ocean is to determine its meaningful geographical, cultural, and political boundaries during different periods in time. Oceans usually serve to mark the frontiers of continents or of historically significant islands, such as the British Isles or Japan, rather than being the subject of historical inquiry on their own. In this book, the first task is to determine what is meant when we speak of the Indian Ocean, so that its history over time can be appreciated.

Like a land mass, an ocean has its own physical characteristics that shape its character and provide the setting for its history. Unlike a continent, an ocean's geography does not consist of plains, mountains, and rivers that determine how men and women traversed it; nor does it possess the kinds of apparent flora and fauna or mineral resources that a land mass provides its human settlers to build society. But oceans do have currents and winds that determine how humans can sail upon their waters, as well as coastlines that connect them to land masses that do possess such resources and settled societies. Oceans also yield protein-rich fish and salt, two of life's real necessities. In the case of the Indian Ocean, it is the way in which these elements combine during different historical periods that give shape and meaning to its history.

As a geographical region, a glance at a globe or an atlas should make it clear that the Indian Ocean is bifurcated on its northern frontier by the Indian subcontinent. This continental intrusion effectively divides the Indian Ocean into two related halves: one dominated on its northwestern side by the Arabian Sea, the other on its northeastern side by the Bay of Bengal. Whether viewed from eastern Africa or Southeast Asia, India is what some scholars have called the fulcrum around which the Indian Ocean gravitates. Over time, however, the Indian Ocean and the coastal world that it washes emerged as a coherent, if multicentered historical unit whose ports were connected by oceanic travel. Nevertheless, the Indian Ocean presents several definitional problems, as a quick reference to different modern maps reveals. First, where does it begin and end? What are its boundaries? How far south does it extend? How far east? Are the Red Sea, the Gulf, the South China Sea part of the Indian Ocean world? Is Australia, which does not enter meaningfully into the region's history until the nineteenth century, to be included? So, we can see right away that even modern maps do not tell us the whole story. The simple answer is that it encompasses everything from the Cape of Good Hope into the Red Sea, across to the South China Sea, and down to Australia, but as one begins to think about the Indian Ocean as a historical region it is useful to keep in mind that both the reality and the idea of the Indian Ocean have changed over time.

Travelers from Polo to Villiers and Holden sailed in vessels that depended upon the winds and currents in a vast oceanic expanse on which men and their ships seemed small and vulnerable. Appreciating how these winds and currents operated in the Indian Ocean is critical to understanding its history. At first, maritime travel was undoubtedly limited to coasting along the shore or across more enclosed bodies of water that are a part of the larger Indian Ocean system, such as the Red Sea, the Gulf, or the Strait of Melaka and the Java Sea in Southeast Asia. For as long as people have inhabited the coastal regions of the Indian Ocean, they have fished its waters, but by and large the range of their vessels was limited. As coastal communities connected over time, however, a pattern of maritime travel by always keeping the coast in sight evolved that continued to predominate even after the evolution of larger sailing vessels. Various kinds of small craft developed locally, with the most complex maritime technology evolving in insular Southeast Asia, which is dominated physically by thousands of islands in close proximity to each other and, in many cases, to the Asian continent. Still, this kind of maritime travel did not make for an oceanic system of transportation and travel. The key discovery that finally made it possible to integrate the Indian Ocean region came sometime in the first millennium

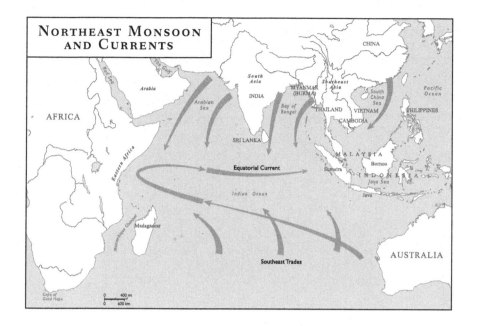

NORTHEAST MONSOON AND CURRENTS

BCE when some unknown Indian Ocean sailors figured out the operation of the seasonal regime of monsoon winds.

The monsoon, a name that appears in similar form in different languages around the rim of the Indian Ocean from East Africa to Indonesia, refers to both the winds and the seasons that accompany these winds. Their regular, predictable appearance semiannually is what makes them so critical for both sailors and farmers who till the lands that surround the oceanic basin. From November through January high pressure builds up over continental Asia and blows dry winds down from Arabia and western India toward eastern Africa and from China toward Southeast Asia. This Northeast Monsoon is accompanied by surface currents that accelerate the movement of ships from north to south around the entire Indian Ocean region, including in the South China Sea.

From April into August this process is reversed, as high pressure zones in the southern hemisphere push strong winds toward the north, once again accompanied by currents that complement the monsoon. The Southwest Monsoon also brings heavy rains to the forested regions of South and Southeast Asia upon which its farmers depend. In general, the Southwest Monsoon blows so strongly in June and July that nearly all dhow sailing was interrupted and some ports in western India and western Malaysia simply closed down during these months. At the same

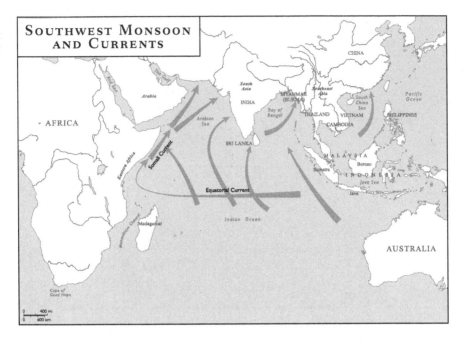

time, even the monsoons could be fickle, as Holden discovered when the dhow on which he sailed was becalmed in the Arabian Sea. "Would the wind ever blow again? You could never tell by looking at the sky. Never knowing when a breeze will stir the sails is the most maddening thing about being becalmed. The never-knowing. One glances at the water— smooth and unruffled; glances at the sails—hanging limply; examines the sky—clear and blue, not a cloud to be seen."

Finally, to Holden's great relief, "After three endless days of stagnation, in the pearly light of an early morning, a fresh breeze filled our sails. We moved!"[8] Sailing the Indian Ocean, as sailing everywhere, was not all romance. Deep knowledge of the winds and currents, hard repetitive work, and luck all played a part in traveling across its waters.

The discovery of this seasonal dramatic shift in the wind regime that dominates the Indian Ocean was the secret to long-distance travel across the breadth of the region, while the very different environments and natural resources that characterize the lands bordering the ocean gave merchants and sailors reason to exchange goods beyond the immediate confines of coasting. The monsoon system did, however, have its limits. Its effect in the western Indian Ocean reached only as far south as the northern Mozambique Channel, where contrary winds and prevailing currents disrupted the ability of ships to make a complete roundtrip from the coasts of southern Africa and Madagascar in a single year.

Likewise, as enclosed seas within the greater Indian Ocean, both the Red Sea—with its prevailing northerly winds from the Gulf of Aqaba to Jidda and its dangerous shoals—and the Gulf—which has its own problems of navigation that include powerful tides—stand at least partially outside the navigational provisions of the monsoons. Similarly, the great distances involved and the regional peculiarities of the monsoons rendered traveling uninterrupted from one extremity of the Indian Ocean world to the other virtually impossible in the era of sail, with South Asia being the obvious location for an intermediary resting point. The existence of several critical choke points that exist within the Indian Ocean also affected travel. Most notably these include the Bab el Mandeb—meaning "Gate of Grief" in Arabic—between the Red Sea and the Gulf of Aden; the Strait of Hormuz, which commands the passage between the Gulf and the Arabian Sea; and the Strait of Melaka, which controlled oceanic movement between the eastern Indian Ocean and the Java Sea, that is, the route linking the Spice Islands and China to the Indian Ocean basin.

In addition, the annual change in the direction of the Equatorial Current influenced how ships sailed the Indian Ocean. During the period of the Northeast Monsoon this current moves west across the Indian Ocean from Australia, skirting across northern Madagascar, and then back in a more northerly stream toward southern Java; during the Southwest Monsoon it runs directly west from Java toward Madagascar and Africa, where it divides both north and south. Although the Equatorial Current was never the preferred way to sail across the Indian Ocean, it may have facilitated Indonesian migration to eastern Africa and Madagascar.

In geological time the current configuration of the Indian Ocean is relatively recent. About fifteen thousand years ago sea levels were some one hundred meters above current levels; ten thousand years ago they were still forty meters above current sea levels. The history explored in this book reaches back perhaps seven thousand years from the present day, when the Indian Ocean attained its current levels. Since then there has been some gradual raising of sea levels and these are now being accelerated by global warming, threatening the very existence of some of the smaller islands in the Indian Ocean, but overall a more or less steady state for this historical period has existed. A rather different environmental feature that has had important effects during this long period is the silting up of certain rivers as a consequence of seasonal flooding, so that over time some seaports became inaccessible from the sea.

To grasp the idea of an Indian Ocean world one needs also to consider the lands that surround the ocean itself. The most meaningful way to do this is to focus on what geographers call the littoral, the coast that links ocean to land. The idea of an Indian Ocean littoral serves as a means to ensure that only those areas of the surrounding land masses that are effectively connected to the Indian Ocean world are included in its history. Geographers suggest one way to determine these linkages is by employing the terms *foreland*, to designate the overseas communities with which a particular coastal settlement or town interacts; *umland*, to indicate the immediate mainland with which the town regularly exchanges goods and shares social relations, including marriage; and *hinterland*, to refer to the mainland zones beyond the umland upon which that settlement draws for its exports and to which its imports are distributed. While the umland will always be circumscribed by the size of the coastal community itself, both the foreland and the hinterland are elastic insofar as both may depend on long-distance trade for its supply of imports and exports. Indeed, relationships based on trade between specific Indian Ocean littorals and hinterlands developed and changed over time.

The basis for any system of exchange is the uneven distribution of both natural and manufactured products. What begins as the simple exchange of local goods produced within different environments, for example, sea salt for agricultural products harvested in the umland, or dried fish in one town for ceramic pots from another, may eventually extend into much wider and deeper forelands and hinterlands. A Tamil poem from south India dating to about two thousand years ago reveals how fishermen produced salt at the coast "where they take fat pearls [salt] from the spreading waves and divide them on the broad shore," to evaporate the water, while a Tamil love poem recounts how salt production already was an engine for coastal and hinterland exchange:

> She is the loving innocent daughter
> of the salt merchant who goes
> through mountain passes in summer
> in his fast bullock cart
> goading his oxen with a stick,
> to sell his white grainy salt,
> made without ploughing in the salt pans,
> near the seashore with a small settlement
> of fishermen who hunt the big ocean
> for fish.[9]

The Indian Ocean is characterized by many such uneven distributions. To take one example, the desert regions of the Horn of Africa and greater

Arabia—the latter rich in dates and pearls, but poor in wood—are flanked by the savannah and forested regions of eastern Africa and western India, both of which have abundant supplies of wood as well as many other desirable goods for exchange, such as ivory from Africa and cotton textiles from India. Similarly, the great attraction of insular Southeast Asia was its precious spices, while China—at the far reaches of the Indian Ocean commercial system—was a major source of silk textiles and other luxury goods. The historical development of these commercial exchanges brought with them in their turn various cultural transformations.

Finally, if the monsoons and currents of the Indian Ocean made it possible to travel across its vastness, and the different products of its surrounding land masses and islands provided a reason to trade such distances, it follows that both people and ideas—ways of thinking and doing—also moved along these watery highways. The inevitable time spent in Indian Ocean ports and on board ships—which themselves formed an essentially male floating society—by sailors, traders, and travelers as they awaited the monsoon encouraged such exchange. Over time these developing social networks nurtured both the evolution of hybrid cultures and cosmopolitan communities. These exchanges and the shifting factors that influenced them form central themes of Indian Ocean history.

One sign of human ingenuity is the varieties of indigenous craft that transported men and their cargoes around and across the Indian Ocean. Before steamships, and today's massive container ships and tankers, seaworthy boats took a variety of forms that evolved over time. The earliest known and most widespread boats from the Indian Ocean region are dugout canoes, probably powered initially by poling, the simplest form of both riverine and coasting vessel. Paddles and oars undoubtedly evolved not long after, as poling could only propel a dugout in shallow waters. Bark boats were a different kind of small craft that were fashioned from trees along parts of the African coast and insular Southeast Asia. Wood rafts are known from the Gulf of Aden and southeast India, but where there were few or no trees, as on the Arabian Peninsula, other natural materials were utilized to construct early boats. Reed boats sealed with bitumen, a form of naturally occurring asphalt, connected the marshlands of southern Iraq to the Arabian shores of the Gulf from as early as circa 5000 BCE. Bladder rafts constructed of inflatable animal skins also existed. While these very different sorts of boats were useful for coasting, none of these small crafts were capable of open sea travel. As larger ships developed, however, and transoceanic voyages linked distant ports together, these smaller boats assumed a new role as lighters to load and unload larger ships where there was no natural harbor and as tugs to guide and sometimes tow big ships that could not navigate by themselves up river deltas or around dangerous shoals.

An early exception to these limitations of size were the large vessels utilized by the ancient Egyptians to sail the Red Sea, although these ships reflect a technology transfer from the Mediterranean and the Nile River rather than from within the Indian Ocean. Most notably there is a panel on the memorial temple to Queen Hatshepsut (r. 1473–58 BCE) at Deir el-Bahri, near Luxor, commemorating the Red Sea voyages she sent to the land of Punt on the Eritrean coast that depicts large galleys with both sails and oars, as well as a side-stern rudder-paddle. These boats probably embarked from Wadi Gawasis, on the Red Sea coast of Egypt, where archaeologists have discovered both coils of rope and the remains of cedar planks. However, there is no evidence that they ever ventured beyond the confines of the Red Sea.

In the western Indian Ocean open seafaring was made possible by the evolution of a category of ship called *dhows*. In fact, this term covers a very broad range of Arab, Indian, and Swahili double-ended keel ships, from small coasting vessels to quite large sea-going ships. Built from the keel up, dhows were carvel-built, that is, planks were laid edge to edge and then sewn together with coir or reed rope, after which they were caulked with bitumen or vegetable matter; no nails were used in construction. The preferred woods used were usually teak or coconut. Deepwater Arab and Indian dhows eventually came to feature construction with a square stern that most scholars believe reflects sixteenth-century Portuguese ship construction, although it is possible that Chinese junk hull design also played a part in this development. Their lateen or roughly triangular sails were set on fore-and-aft, that is, lengthwise from front to back, and were manufactured out of either reed matting or canvas. While lateen sails dominated the open sea shipping of the western Indian Ocean and over to Indonesia, there also existed a type of square-sailed ship in this region. The earliest image of this kind of square-rigged ship is painted on a wall at the Ajanta Caves, a major Buddhist shrine about 200 miles northeast of Mumbai, in western India, that dates to the first half of the sixth century CE. Another example from Mesopotamia of this kind of ship is illustrated in al-Harari's *Maqamat*, which dates to 1237 CE. A third variety of square-rigged boat was the Swahili *mtepe*. The interested tourist can now see a full-scale modern reconstruction of an mtepe in the Zanzibar National Museum. Although these ships used square instead of lateen sails, like dhows they were all constructed with sewn planks.

Among depictions of three different dhows with characteristic lateen sails used in the nineteenth-century East African slave trade there also appears a rectangular-sail mtepe, which represents an older type of sail rigging in the Indian Ocean. The original image appeared in the Illustrated London News, *March 1, 1873.* Courtesy Bodleian Library, University of Oxford

There exists a significant folklore about ships and sailing the sea, an example of which is the poem by the distinguished Swahili poet from Mombasa, Kenya, Ahmed Sheikh Nabhany, written in the traditional heroic *utendi* form with the specific purpose of recounting how to build an mtepe:

> I shall tell you my aim that I have in mind, it is in brief to tell you the story of the ship.
> The *sambo*, you must know, is a vessel built in the past, you must understand, by a prophet, and he was Noah.
> The people of the coast imitated this in their yards, building the useful *mtepe* to carry the cargo.
> The *mtepe*, you must know, was built in Pate by the Bajun folk to enable them to travel.

Daradaki is a tool used in the building, and the fibres of the doum-
palm are pressed in to make a tight joint.
It was beautifully built by skilled craftsmen without the use of nails
but fastened only with cords.
It was sewn with cord—each plank—without any bulge—every crack
being filled so as to leave no space.
The sail was a mat hoisted like an *ushumbi*-sail and the ropes were of
both coir and doum-palm fibres.[10]

In the eastern Indian Ocean three very different categories of sea-
going sailing vessels developed over time: outrigger canoes and their
evolved forms in insular Southeast Asia that are generally grouped together under the name of *perahus*; the Indonesian vessel known as a
jong; and Chinese junks in the South China Sea. Like dhow, perahu
became a catch-all name for many specific types of outrigger canoe
across insular Southeast Asia. Outrigger canoes represent an innovation
to improve the stabilization of dugout canoes and, later, larger sewn,
edge-to-edge plank canoes. They evolved in insular Southeast Asia into
two forms: the double outrigger and the single outrigger. Most authorities agree that the double outrigger is the older form that was pioneered
by Austronesian sailors within the closed Java Sea and that the second
outrigger was abandoned as they ventured farther out into open seas,
where the single outrigger provided greater stability. Early evidence of
outriggers on medium-size ships, rather than canoes, can be found in the
five bas-reliefs at the world's largest Buddhist stupa, a mounded struc-
ture containing sacred relics, at Borodudur, in central Java, which dates
to circa 800 CE. One of the principal pieces of evidence of Austronesian
voyages in the Indian Ocean is the distribution of both types of outrigger in Sri Lanka and southern India, along coastal eastern Africa, in
the Comoros, and at Madagascar. The same maritime technology also
enabled other Austronesian sailors to populate the island world of the
Pacific Ocean.

The largest ship of the Indonesian archipelago, which also appears
to have evolved from the first millennium on, however, was the jong,
which did not have outriggers. Its construction features included dowel
(as distinct from sewn) planking, thereby giving greater rigidity to the
hull; multiple sheathing of the hull for strength; through boards for
additional strength; two side rudders; and unusual rectangular (not
lateen) multiple balance lug sails. Both archaeological and Chinese literary sources provide the evidence for the development of the jong,
while lug sails and side rudders are also illustrated on the Borobudar
reliefs. Like dhows, no iron was used in their construction.

This bas-relief shows that outriggers, square sails, and rear-mounted rudders were all employed on medium-sized ships in insular Southeast Asia. This image is on the port side of the ship at the eighth-century Borobudur stupa in central Java, Indonesia. Mararie, "Ship Relief," September 18, 2012. Photo courtesy of Marieke Kuijjer

The Chinese junk is a very different model for an ocean-going ship. The name possibly derives from the Indonesian word "jong," which itself may come from a Chinese word for "floating house." With origins in the wide, navigable rivers of continental China, ocean-going junks did not begin to appear until late in the first millennium CE.

Junks were flat-bottomed, high-sterned vessels with square bows. Multiple sheathing was common and planks were joined with iron nails and clamps. They utilized two or three masts with lugsails of linen or stiff matting with horizontal battens or strips of wood. The beam of a junk was equal to about one-third the length of the ship and its hull was divided by watertight bulkheads running lengthwise and crosswise. These bulkheads both strengthened the ship and protected it from sinking; they were also valuable for protecting trade goods. As a flat-bottomed boat the junk had no keel, using a steering oar or a single stern-post rudder to stabilize it as it sailed the seas. Of all the premodern ships that sailed the waters of the Indian Ocean, the largest were junks, although their size varied significantly.

One final word about Indian Ocean indigenous shipping concerns the concept of "traditional" culture. While it is true that certain smaller types of boats remained stable right into modern times, so that, for example, simple outrigger canoes can still be seen today along the Mozambique coast, around the Comoros and Madagascar, and in Indonesian lagoons, as well as in the Pacific, larger ocean-going vessels continued to evolve as sailors and shipwrights drew ideas for improvement from other maritime cultures. One example is the technological exchanges implicit in the development of the Indonesian jong and Chinese junk; the arrival of European ships in the Indian Ocean is another, as revealed in the case of the largest Arab and Indian dhows. What is more, the coming of steamships and then motorized boats by no means signaled an immediate end to the viability of these older types of ship.

Just as there were many different types of ships historically, the various sailors of the Indian Ocean world developed and then dispersed different navigational techniques. Understanding the monsoons and currents of the Indian Ocean demanded sophisticated knowledge of the ocean's geography. Coastal sailing required deep knowledge of the topography of the coast and the landmarks by which one sailed, not to mention shoals, sandbars, and tides. In open waters, navigation by the stars and by the technology of Arab science—like the *kamal*, constructed of wood and knotted string to measure the height of the North Star—became important, while Austronesian sailors—who did not share in that technology but could expertly read the stars—were equally skilled at reading oceanic waves. For their part, Chinese sailors also developed important navigational skills and instruments—notably the compass—although most of these were acquired from Persian and Arab captains who came to China. Ibn Majid's *Fawā'id* is the most important navigational text from this premodern era, but by no means is it the only one. After the European invention of the octant around 1730 for calculating celestial navigation, and the subsequent refinement and first manufacture of the sextant in 1757, the latter instrument was also adapted by some Indian Ocean sailors.

Another way humans sought to master the dimensions of the Indian Ocean was through cartography. In about 150 CE the Greek geographer Ptolemy produced a world map that was a major influence on both European and Arab maps for centuries to come. Ptolemy identified two major bodies of water, the Mediterranean Sea and the Indian Ocean, around which the known land masses were situated. He was also the first mapmaker to use longitudinal and latitudinal lines to help locate map positions, even though these were inaccurate. Although Ptolemy left descriptions of the known world, no copies of the original map exist. Eventually, manuscript copies were found in Europe from about 1300, at the beginning of the European era of global exploration, and printed versions began to appear as early as 1477. Without question Ptolemy's world map shows that Europe had possessed a basic notion of the countries of the Indian Ocean basin from the late medieval period. However, the discovery in 2000 of a remarkable cosmological treatise known as the *Book of Curiosities* written by an anonymous Egyptian author sometime between 1020 and 1050 shows that four centuries earlier Arab knowledge of the Indian Ocean world was far superior to that of the West. This astonishing illustrated manuscript includes a rectangular world map that is the first ever to name cities, rather than just regions, among which are included major Indian Ocean ports. A separate Indian Ocean map from the *Book of Curiosities* provides even greater detail of specific places from China to East Africa, including, for example, the Swahili name for the island of Zanzibar,

Both the Red Sea and the Gulf appear clearly, if not entirely accurately, in this Renaissance rendering of Ptolemy's world map by Henrius Martellus Germanus, as do the coastlines around the Arabian Sea. Based on second-century CE knowledge, it shows how Europeans conceptualized the Indian Ocean prior to the Portuguese intrusion at the end of the fifteenth century. Gianni Dagli Orti/The Art Archive at Art Resource, NY, Marine Museum Lisbon

Unguja. Possibly as early as 1389 an unknown Ming cartographer created a world map known as the Da Ming Hun Yi Tu, or Amalgamated Map of the Great Ming Empire, in which Southeast Asia, India, and Africa are represented with varying degrees of accuracy.

Following Portuguese pioneering of the oceanic route around the Cape of Good Hope into the Indian Ocean at the end of the fifteenth century, European knowledge of this vast region increased dramatically. Already a map produced in 1519 by Jorge Reinal shows how quickly the first Portuguese voyages increased Western knowledge of the shape of the Indian Ocean over its representation in Ptolemy's world map. By the time Flemish cartographer Abraham Ortelius published the first world atlas in 1570, the Indian Ocean appears almost in its modern form. Further refinement came at the end of that century in the 1598 map published by Dutch traveler Jan Huyghen van Linschoten. Advances in scientific navigation gradually made possible more refined projection of positions by latitude and longitude, so that the 1750 map by the French royal cartographer Jacques-Nicholas Bellin comes very close to the appearance of modern maps of the Indian Ocean. The final push to map the entire region and its coastlines was an integral part of the expansion of British imperial power in the nineteenth century, while mapping for undersea resources continues today.

Imagining the Indian Ocean world, then, also involves visualizing how it is mapped, as well as factoring in movement across time and space of people, things, and ideas. It further requires appreciating the significance of the thousands of years of historical change from about 5000 BCE to the present that has created a meaningful Indian Ocean world. Weaving these very different perspectives together makes it possible to imagine an Indian Ocean world that makes sense historically and contemporaneously.

The Ancient Indian Ocean

The anonymous author of the *Periplus of the Erythraen Sea*, the first-century CE commercial guide to the major trading ports of the western Indian Ocean for merchants of imperial Rome, described the port of Muza, located at the southern end of the Red Sea, somewhere near the modern port of Mocha, in Yemen, with these words: "The whole place teems with Arabs—ship owners or charters and sailors—and is astir with commercial activity. For they share in the trade across the water and with Barygaza, using their own outfits."[1] This beehive of maritime commercial activity was linked to both the facing African coast and out beyond the Bab el Mandeb to the ancient predecessor of Broach or Bharuch, later the most important port of southern Gujarat in India. How these oceanic connections were forged is the focus of this chapter. It explores the different historical developments that over several millennia eventually coalesced into a coherent trading network that spanned the full geographical extent of the Indian Ocean world, from eastern Africa to China.

The evidence for this evolution is diffuse and often opaque, but by stitching together multiple sources from across the broad region, historians have discerned how an oceanic system emerged over time from coasting trade and short open sea communication at the edges of the ocean. One problem in reconstruction, however, is that the sources are largely derived from research on and the observations of various states and empires that focused primarily on continental Asia and Africa and for which sea-going trade was of secondary importance. Furthermore, the voices of ordinary coast dwellers and sailors, or even traders, are silent during this long period. So interpretation of these sources must be tempered at all times by remaining alert to the kinds of coasting activities by ordinary people that unquestionably contributed to the making of the commercial networks that created an Indian Ocean world.

Navigation across the northern rim of the Indian Ocean may date to as early as about 5000 BCE. This achievement was neither centralized

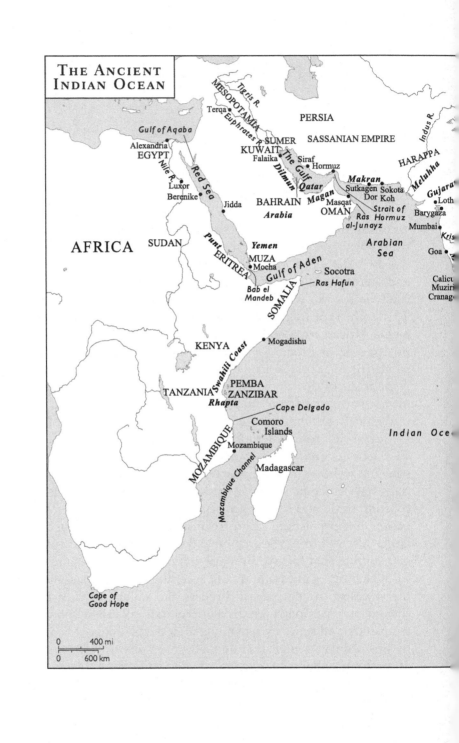

THE ANCIENT
INDIAN OCEAN

Tigris R.

MESOPOTAMIA

Euphrates R.

Terqa

PERSIA

SASSANIAN EMPIRE

Indus R.

Gulf of Aqaba

Alexandria
EGYPT

SUMER

KUWAIT
Falaika

The Gulf

Dilmun

Siraf
Hormuz

HARAPPA

Meluhha

Luxor
Berenike

Red Sea

Nile R.

Jidda

Qatar

BAHRAIN

Magan

Masqat

Arabia

OMAN

Makran

Sutkagen
Dor Koh

Sokota

Gujarat

Loth

Strait of
Ras Hormuz
al-Junayz

Barygaza

Mumbai

AFRICA

SUDAN

Punt

ERITREA

Yemen

MUZA
Mocha

Gulf of Aden

Arabian
Sea

Kris

Goa

Socotra

Bab el
Mandeb

Ras Hafun

SOMALIA

Calicu
Muziri
Cranag

KENYA

Swahili Coast

Mogadishu

TANZANIA

Rhapta

PEMBA

ZANZIBAR

Cape Delgado

Comoro
Islands

Indian Oce

MOZAMBIQUE

Mozambique

Mozambique Channel

Madagascar

Cape of
Good Hope

0   400 mi

0   600 km

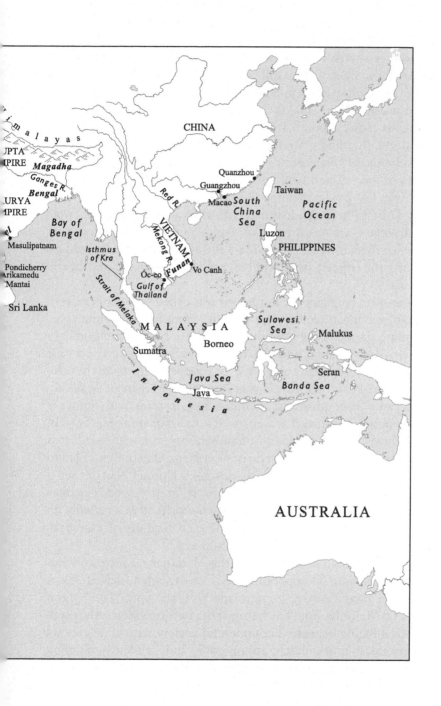

CHINA

Quanzhou
Guangzhou
Taiwan
Macao
South
China
Sea
Pacific
Ocean

Red R.

VIETNAM

Mekong R.

Óc-eo
Funan
Vo Canh
Gulf of
Thailand

Luzon

PHILIPPINES

Isthmus
of Kra

Bay of
Bengal

Masulipatnam

Pondicherry
Arikamedu
Mantai

Sri Lanka

Magadha

Ganges R.

Bengal

GUPTA
EMPIRE

MAURYA
EMPIRE

H i m a l a y a s

Strait of Melaka

MALAYSIA

Sumatra

Borneo

Sulawesi
Sea

Malukus

Seran

Java Sea
Java

Banda Sea

I n d o n e s i a

AUSTRALIA

nor dependent on great civilizations, but constructed over time by local and regional coasting exchanges in the Arabian Sea, the Gulf, and the Red Sea. The earliest evidence that speaks to this trade is the discovery of Ubaid pottery sherds from Mesopotamia that archaeologists found along the western side of the Gulf, indicating exchange networks of fisherfolk in the Gulf. Although Sumerian migration from about 4000 BCE created a centralized state in Mesopotamia, this rich agricultural area of what is today modern Iraq lacked certain basic materials like wood and stone. Building upon the same maritime network that facilitated the exchange of Ubaid pottery, Sumerian merchants at first traded with an area of the Arabian Gulf lying between Falaika, in Kuwait, and Qatar that was known to them as Dilmun. Eventually, because of its safe harbor, Dilmun became identified with Bahrain Island. Grain, pottery, and bitumen—a natural form of asphalt used for caulking reed boats, evidence for which dates to circa 5500 BCE—were exchanged by the Sumerians for copper, stone, timber, tin, dates, onions, and pearls from the Gulf.

In the Sumerian language the Euphrates was called "the copper river" and Dilmun merchants traded upriver to major cities like Ur. Dilmun was not the ultimate source of many of these materials, but the intermediary port between Mesopotamia and the farther reaches of the northwest Indian Ocean. Stone, especially alabaster, and copper came from the interior of the Oman Peninsula, which was known as Magan or Makkan, while wood came from northwestern India. Magan trade with Sumer is attested to by pottery imports that were used in cairn or stone pile burials. Accounts of the Akkadian conqueror of Sumer, Sargon I, who ruled circa 2400 BCE, refer to an unidentified style of boat from Magan that sailed to his empire, while another source clearly describes Dilmun boats as sewn plank boats. Although both Mesopotamia and Dilmun viewed Magan as part of the wild, peripheral part of the known world, it was actually an important maritime link to the Indus Valley civilization of Harappa, which archaeologists date to circa 2600–1900 BCE.

Harappa was known as Meluhha to the Akkadians. Like the evolution of state-building in Mesopotamia, its focus was land-based, but it also engaged in significant sea-going trade with the Gulf. The Sargon I text refers to Meluhha boats as being large cargo vessels. Although Harappa was a highly organized commercial society with state control of artisan production, its merchants operated independently. Trading colonies were located at or near the coast at Lothal, in Gujarat, and Sutkagen Dor and Sokta Koh on the Makran coast of modern Pakistan. These were all fortified settlements between the coast and its hinterland.

Decorated Ubaid pottery from the fifth millennium BCE *was used domestically as drinking and serving vessels in Mesopotamia. Similar pottery was traded from Mesopotamia into the western Gulf.* Erich Lessing/Art Resource, NY, ART203237

Harappan goods that reached the Gulf included pots that probably carried ghee or clarified butter, ritual axe blades used in burials, carnelian beads, wood, and seals and weights. In fact, Harappan seals influenced the style of Gulf seals and Harappan weights became the standard weights in the Gulf. Ships sailing from this part of the northwestern Indian Ocean to the Gulf and beyond to Africa undoubtedly followed the coastline, but they also ventured from Sutkagen Dor across the open sea to Ras al-Junayz at the easternmost tip of the Arabian Peninsula in Oman, where 20 percent of archaeological finds are from Harappa. It seems likely that this bleak landmark had become a waystation in an emerging Indian Ocean system of exchange.

The ancient Red Sea represents a much more self-contained exchange system than does that of the Mesopotamia to Harappa circuit. Pharaonic voyages to the land of Punt, now clearly identified as the coast of Sudan and Eritrea, date to circa 2600–1150 BCE, that is, contemporary to the development of sea links between the Gulf and the Indus Valley. Early evidence for Red Sea trade to the Nile Valley includes burials with

This set of standardized graduated weights, each cut from a different stone, comes from Harappa. Such weights were also adopted for trade in the ancient Gulf. Copyright 1996–2008, J. M. Kenoyer/Harappa.com, courtesy Department of Archaeology and Museums, Government of Pakistan

Indian Ocean cowrie shells, as well as references to exotic trade goods from Punt, including myrrh, incense, and ebony. The example of Queen Hatshepsut's voyages in the mid-second millennium BCE may have arisen from a royal decision to take a new initiative in the Red Sea trade. According to a panel celebrating the success of her Punt expeditions on her memorial temple, the god of Amun declared to her:

> I have given to thee all Punt as far as the lands of the gods of God's-Land.
>
> No one trod the Myrrh-terraces, which the people knew not; it was heard of from mouth to mouth by hearsay of the ancestors—. The marvels brought thence under thy fathers, the Kings of Lower Egypt, were brought from one to another, and since the time of the ancestors of the Kings of Upper Egypt, who were of old, as a return for many payments; none reaching them except thy carriers.
>
> But I will cause thy army to tread them, I have led them on water and on land, to explore the waters of inaccessible channels, and I have reached the Myrrh-terraces.[2]

Hatshepsut's impressive initiative apparently did not outlast her personal reign, but Red Sea trade, even if it did not connect with the wider Indian Ocean at this time, certainly persisted.

By about 2000 BCE there is, however, fascinating ethnobotanical, archaeological, and linguistic evidence that the three northwest Indian

Ocean subregions—Red Sea, Gulf, Indus Valley—had indeed already overlapped. Botanical evidence derives from scientific analysis of the exchange of plants and animals between Africa, Arabia, and South Asia. These exchanges around the rim of the northwestern Indian Ocean depended on small-scale trade in the hands of coastal fishing communities rather than the more dramatic luxury trade that was driven by land-based states. Indeed, the absence or decline of major states in this period emphasizes the point that historians must not overlook small-scale contributions to the making of an Indian Ocean world.

What this evidence suggests is that from about 2200 BCE a major climate shift that created a drier and less predictable environment sustained the movement of domesticated crops from the northern savannah regions of Africa to their counterparts in India along routes that skirted the northern coastline of the Arabian Sea. Among these African crops that migrated to South Asia are three cereals—sorghum (*Sorghum bicolor*), pearl millet (*Pennisetum glaucum*), and finger millet (*Eleusine coracana*); many varieties of cowpea (*Vigna unguiculata*); and hyacinth bean (*Lablab purpueus*).

Although these food crops are now widely distributed on the Indian subcontinent, their earliest appearance comes from the Late Harappan period, dating to circa 1900–1300 BCE. Each of these African crops was additional to endemic Indian crops, which may account for their ready adoption by Indian farmers. What is interesting is that there are no reliable reports of any African crops being adopted on the Arabian Peninsula during this early period, although sorghum, pearl millet, finger millet, and the African peas and beans, as well as the Ethiopian cereal tef (*Eragrostis tef*) all reached Arabia by the last centuries before the Current Era. There is evidence, too, that common or broomcorn millet (*pannicum miliaceum*), a cereal of Chinese origin, eventually migrated across South Asia and Arabia to northeast Africa, probably by sea, as early as the period 2000–1500 BCE. According to genetic evidence, the most important food-source contribution from India to Africa by sea, as opposed to land, was the zebu cow (*Bos indicus*), although the timing and distribution of its appearance in Africa is widely varied. Unlike cereals, which can be transported unintentionally, but like legumes, the movement of livestock reveals human intentionality. Certain weeds and rodents—black rat, house mouse, and house shrew, the latter all going from India to Africa—also reflect unintentional seaborne exchanges across the northwest Indian Ocean.

The societies of the eastern Indian Ocean were still taking shape during these millennia with the maritime peopling of insular—meaning islands—and parts of peninsular Southeast Asia by Austronesian-speaking people taking center stage. This widely dispersed Austronesian language family, which extends spatially from Madagascar in the southwestern Indian Ocean to Hawaii and Easter Island in the Pacific Ocean, is intimately linked to the sea. Linguists have established that Taiwan Island was the original home of this remarkable language family and that from about 3000 BCE pioneering speakers began the long process of populating the islands and coasts of modern Indonesia, Micronesia, and Polynesia. The first move from Taiwan was probably to Luzon Island, in the northern Philippines, a migration that was obviously carried out in boats. In fact, historical linguistic reconstruction of this proto-language indicates the use of canoes, as well as a number of tropical food crops.

After groups of men and women established themselves as settlers on any particular island, other adventurers moved out to explore the maritime frontier. For the Malayo-Polynesian branch of Austronesian that today dominates maritime Southeast Asia, the islands of the Sulawesi Sea, in the eastern reaches of Indonesia, may have been a major dispersal zone from as early as about 1500 BCE, but this process continued right into the first century CE. Although the archaeological record is incomplete, it generally supports the very clear linguistic evidence for this extraordinary process of human migration. We must assume that these thousands of islands, both large and small, were either uninhabited or so sparsely inhabited that there was no resistance to the new languages that these maritime settlers spoke. The one area of this vast oceanic region that did resist the expansion of Austronesian languages is New Guinea, which was a center of primary agricultural development and had a population density that created a barrier to the adoption of these new languages. The joining together of the very different worlds of the eastern and western Indian Ocean was now possible with the settlement of the islands of Southeast Asia by Austronesian speakers.

By the late centuries BCE the vast area inhabited by speakers of Malayo-Polynesian languages was marked by what scholars refer to as an "oceanic nomadism." These expert sailors had learned to navigate by reading wave and swell patterns, cloud formations, winds, and the animal life they observed both above and below the water. Archaeological evidence from a wide range of sites reveals that Malay sailors carried pottery from Vietnam throughout the region in the middle half of the first millennium BCE. They also carried the Dong Son bronze ceremonial drums from the Red River Valley and coast of northern Vietnam, where they were manufactured, as far as peninsular Malaysia, the large islands

This Dong Son brass drum, which dates from the third to first centuries BCE, *is decorated with a characteristic twelve-point star design. Similar drums from northern Vietnam were traded extensively across maritime Southeast Asia.* Erich Lessing/Art Resource, NY, ART90499

of Sumatra and especially Java, and as far east as several locations around the Banda Sea. Some of these drums depict warriors in long boats. Whereas Austronesian expansion had been by coasting, the trade relations that linked northern Vietnam to insular Southeast Asia is strong evidence that Malay sailors had now discovered the operation of the monsoon in the South China Sea. Further testimony to their mastery of the monsoon comes from Chinese records of the third century BCE that mention Malay sailors from the "Kunlun" islands, which they accurately describe as being volcanic and mysterious. Although Chinese sources suggest that "Kunlun" was variously applied to denote "otherness" and "blackness," including Malays and Africans, in this context it seems most likely to apply to the island world of Southeast Asia.

A century earlier, to the west, Alexander the Great's land-based conquests in Asia Minor extended Greek influence from the eastern Mediterranean to India. His armies also established numerous new port cities throughout the region and opened up the western Indian Ocean to Greek merchants, shipping, and cultural influences. The city of Alexandria, Egypt, which Alexander the Great founded in 331 BCE, soon became central to the opening up of the Red Sea to rapidly growing Indian Ocean trade. At about the same time Alexander's fleet commander Nearchus planted a Greek colony at Falaika Island in the northwestern corner of the Gulf as part of his commander's ultimately disastrous march to the Indus. Today a visitor to Kuwait can see the remains of a Greek temple, while archaeologists have also excavated numerous Greek pottery shards there.

In 275 BCE Ptolemy II of Egypt founded a port on the western coast of the Red Sea at the boundary of the Eastern Desert of Egypt and named it after his mother, Berenike I. Located inside a natural harbor that is protected by a peninsula, Berenike was designed to bring African war elephants to Egypt since the Seleucid Persians had blocked the overland routes for acquiring Indian war elephants. More generally, during the period of the Ptolemy rulers of Egypt, Greek traders called Yavanas in Indian Ocean sources became active as far east as Sri Lanka, while Greek ideas and culture left a major imprint on many regional societies. From the perspective of the Mediterranean world the most important development of this era was the first-century BCE "discovery" by the Greek navigator Hippalus of the operation of the Southwest Monsoon, which enabled ships leaving the Red Sea and entering the Arabian Sea to sail directly to India.

The Roman conquest of Ptolemaic Egypt in 30 BCE proved to be a further stimulus to trade between the ancient Mediterranean and Indian Ocean worlds. During the first century CE Alexandria prospered as the principal Indian Ocean trading emporium for the Mediterranean, while Berenike flourished like never before. The *Periplus of the Erythraen Sea* dates to this period of expansive Roman trade. Berenike figures as one of the major trading ports mentioned in the *Periplus*, a fact that is borne out by extensive archaeological excavations at the now-abandoned site that reveal the presence of trade goods from across the Indian Ocean world. Spices, myrrh, frankincense, pearls, textiles from China, and glass beads from both India and East Java have been identified, as well as ivory and large amounts of teak from India that was probably recycled from ships. Numerous amphoras for carrying many of these goods, no doubt as well as ghee and oils, were also excavated. Perhaps most telling is the discovery of the largest single find in the ancient world of Indian black pepper, weighing some sixteen pounds. A vivid example of the cosmopolitan influences that came together at Berenike from disparate points connected to the Indian Ocean world are two very different representations of the goddess Aphrodite/Venus and graffiti—the literature of the common person—written in South Arabian, Palmyrene, Axumite, and Tamil-Brahmi, all found at Berenike.

The rise of the Achaemenid dynasty in Persia in the sixth century BCE marks the beginning of a new era in the western Indian Ocean world, one that is dominated by a new set of Gulf states and their conquerors and that ultimately led to the initial integration of the entire Indian Ocean littoral. But the Persian Empire in its successive iterations was land-based and only peripherally interested in its maritime borders. Meanwhile, those who inhabited those coastal borders continued to exchange goods and ideas according to their own needs. The most important impact of the rise of the Persian Empire, its defeat by Alexander the Great in 330 BCE, and the sequence of its subsequent dynasties—the Seleucids, Parthians, and especially Sassanians—was to reinvigorate and shift the focus of trade in the Gulf from its western to its eastern shores, from the Arabian to the Persian side. As a consequence, new ports arose and new commodities entered Indian Ocean commerce, such as different brocades and carpets, pearls, and horses. In addition, wars with imperial Rome and Byzantium restricted overland trade in the first centuries CE and consequently emphasized the value of sea-borne trade for both the Persians and Romans. The Persians now established several secure maritime ports of trade in the wider Gulf.

According to a Middle Persian text, when Ardasir I, founder of the Sassanian Empire in 224 CE, "saw the ocean before his eyes, he offered thanksgiving to God, called that place the city [modern Bushire] of *Bokht Ardashir* ['saved by Ardashir'], and ordered an Atash-I Warharan ['victorious fire'] to be enthroned on that sea-coast,"[3] as the coast had provided refuge from his enemies during his struggle against the last Parthian king. A century later the port of Siraf emerged as a major seaport, while the town of Old Hormuz on the south coast of Iran was strategically positioned to guard the narrow entrance to the Gulf. Located on the opposite coast of the Strait of Hormuz, the Persians under King Xusro I, who ruled from 531 to 579, established Masqat to service the trade from India to Aden and thence up into the Red Sea.

Parallel to these changes in the Gulf was the emergence of new states in South Asia following the end of the Harappan civilization and the rise of new ports on both coasts of the Indian subcontinent. The most important early state was Magadha, on the Ganges River Plain in northern India, which took shape from the seventh century BCE. In the wake of Alexander's failed invasion of India in 326 BCE, Chandragupta Maurya seized the Magadha throne and established the Gupta Empire that lasted to 185 BCE. His grandson, Asoka, who reigned for sixty years from 272 to 232 BCE, extended the Mauryan Empire to southern India while the rise of both Buddhism and Jainism as major religions, with their emphasis on individual achievement and personal salvation, fostered the development of commerce. At the same time, Asoka's vigorous promotion of Buddhism encouraged overseas trade. Eventually South Asian traders established outposts as far abroad as Socotra Island off the Horn of Africa, at Alexandria, and in Southeast Asia, while both Greek and Persian traders were carving out important roles in South Asian trade.

The major South Asian ports named in the *Periplus* provide much evidence of the diversity and importance of this trade, which now intimately linked the Mediterranean world to that of the northwestern Indian Ocean. The most important coastal emporium of northwestern India was Barygaza (modern Bharuch), upstream from the mouth of the Narmada River in South Gujarat. The major port of the Malabar littoral of southwestern India was Muziris, probably Pattanam, while Arikamedu, which is also referred to as Yavana or "Greeks" in Tamil literature, was its counterpart on the Coromandel coast of southeast India. Masalia, the predecessor of Masulipatnam at the Krishna delta, was a busy port on the Bay of Bengal; Mantai, on the northwestern coast of Sri Lanka, was the major transshipment point linking the exchange of goods between the eastern and western Indian Ocean. All of these towns trace their origins to the last centuries before the Current Era and each was connected to the continental trade of an inland-based state.

The *Periplus* provides abundant detail on the goods exchanged at each port, citing grains, metals, timber, various luxury goods, beads, and textiles as important categories of South Asian exports, with specie—coins of every sort in all precious metals—the dominant import. Both the *Periplus* and archaeological evidence reveal that wine, olive oil, and fish sauce were transported in amphoras, but these items were probably destined mainly for Greek and Roman colonies in India. Thus, as early as the first century of the Current Era there is clear evidence that South Asian exports were greater than its imports, which led to a constant drain on Western sources of precious metals and bullion and, after discovery of the New World, drove the European search for silver and gold mines.

Although luxury trade dominates the available sources, the international trade also provided opportunities for common folk who inhabited the regions around these major ports. According to the author of the *Periplus* writing about the mouth of the Narmada River, "This gulf which leads to Barygaza, since it is narrow, is hard for vessels coming from seaward to manage. . . . For this reason local fishermen in the king's service come out with crews [sc. of rowers] and long ships, the kind called *trappaga* and *kotymba*, to the entrance as far as Syrastrênê to meet vessels and guide them up to Barygaza." He comments on the "extreme ebb-and-flood tides" that rendered most Indian river deltas dangerous, but especially that of Barygaza, where the rush of water during flood tides made "something like the rumble of an army heard from afar." He continues, "Thus the navigating of ships in and out is dangerous for those who are inexperienced and are entering this port of trade for the first time. For, once the thrust of the flood tide is under way, restraining anchors do not stay in place. Consequently, the ships, carried along by its force and driven sideways by the swiftness of the current, run aground on the shoals and break up, while smaller craft even capsize." Clearly, without the skill of local pilot ships Barygaza could not have become a usable port for Indian Ocean trade. As the author of the *Periplus* explains, "Through the crew's efforts, they maneuver them right from the mouth of the gulf through the shoals and tow them to predetermined stopping places; they get them under way when the tide comes in and, when it goes out, bring them to anchor in certain harbors and basins."[4]

Roman historian Pliny the Elder comments in his *Natural History* on another danger to trading in the Indian Ocean: pirates. Writing about the discovery of a shorter route to India, he notes that "the voyage is made every year, with companies of archers on board, because these seas used to be very greatly infested by pirates." Since the definition of piracy and pirates is very much in the eye of the beholder and reflects the dynamics of commercial sea power, we cannot know for certain how these "pirates" regarded their maritime activities. In any case, Pliny advises his readers not to head for Cranagore, on the Malabar coast, which he depicts as "not a desirable port of call, on account of the neighbouring pirates," while adding "furthermore the roadstead for shipping is a long way from the land and cargoes have to be brought in and carried out by boats." Speaking next of the small port of Barace at the far southwestern tip of the Indian subcontinent, Pliny notes that "pepper is conveyed to Barace in canoes made of hollowed tree-trunks."[5] Here, in this incidental line, one again glimpses how ordinary people contributed to the now-flourishing international trade of the Indian Ocean. Perhaps some of this pepper was even sent to Berenike.

The most important archaeological site for Roman trade in India, however, is Arikamedu, known to both Romans and Greeks as Poduke. Located about three kilometers south of Pondicherry in southeast India, Arikamedu's origins date to circa 200 BCE–200 CE but are clearly pre-Roman. Its fame derives from its production of drawn, that is, cut from a tube, glass trade beads, which as early as the first century BCE had appeared in Indonesia. From there production spread across Southeast Asia, possibly through the agency of a powerful guild. The artisans of Arikamedu also produced stone beads and innovated black onyx and citrine beads. The beads of Arikamedu connect it directly to Roman Berenike, where archaeologists have excavated hundreds of these beads.

Looking eastward from southern India at this period we find a maritime commercial world dominated by Malay shipping. In addition to their extraordinary maritime skills, Malay traders controlled some of the most desired commodities in the ancient world: spices. The focal point of the spice trade was the Maluku Islands, a small archipelago at the far eastern frontier of Indonesia. Before 1600 CE cloves, the dried unopened flower bud of the clove tree, grew only on five tiny volcanic islands off the western coast of Halmahera; nutmeg, the kernel inside the seed, and mace, the rind that covers the kernel, of the mace-nutmeg tree grew exclusively on a tiny group of ten islands covering a total area of seventeen square miles south of Seram Island. These spices were the product of a highly skilled arboriculture that the indigenous islanders and Javanese traders did not want to share with outsiders. Some of these spices were known as rare precious items in the Ancient Middle East, which they reached no doubt through a very indirect process of exchanges. The earliest known evidence dates to the discovery of a few carbonized cloves at the site of Terqa, in modern Syria, that are radiocarbon-dated to 1721 BCE. Cloves are also mentioned in an early second-century CE medical text from Kushan in northwestern India and by fourth-century Gupta court poets. Eventually they became an especially lucrative element in the Indian Ocean trade of Southeast Asia.

In addition, Malays traded cinnamon from south China to the western Indian Ocean, probably indirectly at first, but possibly directly over time. Cinnamon was certainly known to the ancient Egyptians, who used it medicinally and in funerary rituals, but the fact that there are many different varieties of cinnamon makes it impossible to associate it with Austronesian traders at this early period. More to the point, the ancient Greek sources leave no doubt that the cinnamon known to them came from either Somalia or Arabia. Writing in the first century CE Pliny mentions "rafts" used by cinnamon traders between Asia and Africa who sailed "from gulf to gulf," no doubt taking advantage of the monsoon.[6] Although some scholars believe that these "rafts" were actually outrigger canoes, there is no evidence to sustain such a reading of this source, which actually corroborates the northwest Indian Ocean origins of this sought-after spice. To be sure, the Greek word for cinnamon derives from a Malayo-Polynesian word and in later periods the tree itself spread across the Indian Ocean. Indirect evidence from a thirteenth-century Arab text mentions Malays settled in south Arabia at the time of the Roman conquest of Egypt in 31 BCE. In light of other evidence, this assertion seems quite possible.

Spices were not, however, the only resources that attracted outsiders to Southeast Asia. It was also an important, almost mythical, source of gold. Indian sources from the first centuries of the Current Era refer to Southeast Asia as the Yavadvipa, "Golden Island" or "Golden Peninsula," as does Ptolemy writing in about 150 CE. As the intermediary between China and South Asia, its maritime traders also carried silk, for which there was a huge demand in the Mediterranean world, across the Indian Ocean. Not surprisingly, like the spices of the Malukus, silkworms were jealously guarded in China before some were smuggled to Byzantium in the mid-sixth century CE.

The pivotal region of Southeast Asia for the trade connecting China to India and points west was an area known only by its Chinese name of Funan. In the third century CE, Funan expanded from its inland capital of Vyadhapura down to the Gulf of Thailand and Malay Peninsula as far as the Isthmus of Kra. Indian Ocean traders reached Funan by portaging across the narrow Isthmus of Kra then sailing across the Gulf of Thailand to the coastal plain where a series of canals moved goods to Vyadhapura. Although this commerce was pioneered by Malay and then Indian traders, by the second century CE both Arab and Greek traders had reached Funan. In 166 CE two probably Greek merchants traveling by way of Funan reached China, where they boldly claimed to be emissaries from Roman Emperor Marcus Aurelius. In the middle of the following century an envoy named Kang Tai from the kingdom of Wu in southern China reached Funan. In the words of Kang Tai, in Funan: "There is a saying [that] in foreign countries there are three abundances, the abundance of men in China, the abundance of precious things in Da Qin [the Roman West], and the abundance of horses among the Yuezhi," a Central Asian people who inhabited the Kushan Empire of northern South Asia.[7]

By this time it appears that the Chinese had learned of the Indian Ocean monsoons that enabled ships to travel "with the seasonal wind" from South India to the Gulf.[8] Archaeologists working at the Funan port of Óc-eo, on the Mekong delta of Vietnam near the border with Cambodia, have found imports from India, Persia, and the Mediterranean, as well as local manufactures. An important element of the India trade to China during this period was dominated by horse traders from Kushana, who moved their charges down the Ganges River plain to Bengal, where archaeologists have found terra-cotta seals depicting Kushana horse traders. This traffic reveals a remarkable example of how demand for an important item of maritime trade in the Indian Ocean at this time—horses from northwest India—reached deep into the hinterland of the Bengal ports from which they were loaded onto ships to be transported by sea to Funan and, finally, to China. No doubt it was along this route in reverse that cloves reached the Kushan and Gupta courts in these centuries.

The exotic finds at Óc-Eo include gold medallions with Roman images, as well as Hindu images from India and Buddhist statuettes from China. Tin amulets carrying symbols of the Hindu gods Visnu and Siva point to the growing importance of these two Hindu deities in Southeast Asia, where ambitious local rulers initially sought to enhance their own authority by embracing them. The way in which the rulers of Funan seized upon Indic ideologies reflects the process of Indianization that marked much of Southeast Asia in the first millennium CE. At the same time, inspired by South Asian images of the Buddha, Funan artists developed a new style of representation that is preserved in several graceful freestanding wooden Buddhas. By the early sixth century this style could be seen at several Funan sites in stone statues depicting both Buddhist images and Visnu. Beyond Funan, inscriptions in the ancient Indian language of Sanskrit exist from about 400 CE in west Kalamantan, on Borneo, and fifty years later in west Java, as well as at Vo Canh (modern Nha Trang) on the east coast of Vietnam, where people were Malay-speaking. In fact, both Hinduism and Buddhism exerted powerful cultural influence in Southeast Asia, although it is clear that the region's people integrated these influences and shaped them to their own spiritual needs, as they later did with Islam.

From its roots in the Ganges plain of northern India, Buddhism eventually spread to Sri Lanka, which became a major center for subsequent missionary activity back up the Bay of Bengal to coastal India. The Buddhist tradition of pilgrimage encouraged movement within the Buddhist world, while Buddhist missionaries and merchants were active in insular Southeast Asia by the middle of the fourth century CE. A particularly well-known figure was the royal Kashmiri monk Gunavarman, who reached Java from Sri Lanka in the early 420s and whose renown took him to China, where he died at the Song court after establishing an order of Buddhist nuns there. According to Hui-Chiao's "Lives of Eminent Monks," the day before Gunavarman reached Java from Sri Lanka, the mother of the Javanese king dreamed that she had seen a holy man arrive in a flying boat. One way to interpret this passage is to recognize it as a symbol of the regular seaborne communication that existed between South and Southeast Asia within the sacred geography of Buddhism. A fascinating development within Buddhism during this period was the emergence of the cult of a savior from the perils of travel by both land and sea. The earliest evidence for the latter practices dates to a second- to first-century BCE medallion from Bharut, in Madhya Pradesh, India, which shows a sea monster about to swallow a boat in distress while its inscription relates how a merchant named Vasugupta looked to the Buddha to save him.

The earliest presence of South Asians in Southeast Asia, which they reached by coasting and overland, dates to the first millennium BCE. By the time the monk Gunavarman had reached Java, however, Malay sailors had already pioneered the all-sea route between these two Indian Ocean subregions. The key to this discovery was their mastery of the monsoon regime and navigation of the Strait of Melaka, which allowed ships to avoid the delay of overland passage across the Isthmus of Kra. Sailing by this route also made ports in Java and, eventually, Sumatra the principal transit points for those traveling on to China.

The first written account of this route is the Buddhist monk Făxiăn's *A Record of the Buddhist Countries*, which dates to 414 CE. Făxiăn began his journey from a monastery in China over the Himalayas to the Ganges River Plain in 399 at the age of sixty-five, wandering as a pilgrim and collecting sacred texts before traveling on to Sri Lanka, which was by then a major Buddhist culture with more than 5,000 monks. Finally, in about 411 he decided to return to China by sea. According to his account, "he took passage in a large merchantman, on board of which there were more than 200 men. . . . With a favourable wind, they proceeded eastwards for three days, and then they encountered a great wind. The vessel sprang a leak and the water came in." The merchants with whom Făxiăn traveled all feared for their lives, so they threw their goods overboard, as did the monk with his simple earthly possessions. He refused, however, to discard the sacred Buddhist books and images he had collected over his time in India and Sri Lanka, calling upon the Buddha to save him and his companions, "Let me, by your dread and supernatural (power), return from my wanderings, and reach my resting-place!"

After almost two weeks of storm the ship reached shore and the leak was plugged. The tempest was not, however, the end of the travelers' travails, as Făxiăn writes:

> On the sea (hereabouts) there are many pirates, to meet with whom is speedy death. The great ocean spreads out, a boundless expanse. There is no knowing east or west; only by observing the sun, moon, and stars was it possible to go forward. If the weather were dark and rainy, (the ship) went as she was carried by the wind, without any definite course. In the darkness of the night, only the great waves were to be seen, breaking on one another, and emitting a brightness like that of fire, with huge turtles and other monsters of the deep (all about). The merchants were full of terror, not knowing where they were going. The sea was deep and bottomless, and there was no place where they could drop anchor and stop. But when the sky became clear, they could tell east and west, and (the ship) again went forward in the right direction.[9]

Făxiăn leaves no doubt in the reader's mind as to the perils of sailing the open seas, both natural and human. While his account does not specify exactly where these pirates based their operations, the Strait of Melaka and the islands at either entrance to it comprise one of the most notorious oceanic passages for piracy in the world. It also speaks indirectly to the skill of navigating by the stars and sun once the sky became visible. In the end, after sailing for many weeks, Făxiăn's ship reached Java. After resting there for five months Făxiăn continued his journey on a large merchant ship to China, which reached its destination only after another major storm at sea pushed it beyond its intended port.

There remain two other major historical processes for this era that demand attention: first, the expansion of Bantu-speaking people along coastal East Africa and across to the Comoro Islands and, second, the peopling of Madagascar by Austronesian-speaking people. The author of the *Periplus* writes about the African coast beyond Ras Hafun, at the easternmost tip of the Horn of Africa, identifying its most important and southerly port of trade by the name of Rhapta, after its sewn boats, certainly ancestral to the *mtepe*. He notes, too, that the coast was under the domination of a South Arabian king and that ivory was the main item of trade from Rhapta. Unfortunately, although Roman artifacts have been unearthed around the delta of the Rufiji River in modern mainland Tanzania, no one has successfully identified the location of Rhapta, which must have been somewhere along this stretch of the coast. It is not clear whether the people of Rhapta were Bantu-speaking ancestors of the Swahili people who came to dominate coastal East

Africa. What is evident archaeologically is that the people of the coast possessed sufficient maritime skills to traverse the dangerous immediate oceanic foreland and to populate its offshore islands.

Whether the people of Rhapta were Bantu speakers or not, both archaeological and historical linguistic evidence leave no doubt that the proto-Swahili speakers spread rapidly from a homeland in the coastal hinterland of Kenya down the coast south beyond Cape Delgado, the promontory that marks the boundary between Tanzania and Mozambique. Eventually settlers from this language group sailed across the northern Mozambique Channel to populate the Comoro Islands, where dialects of Comorian are all closely related to Swahili. The archaeological record closely parallels this linguistic expansion, although without written evidence, like the graffiti found at Berenike, the makers of ancient artifacts cannot be identified linguistically. Nevertheless, the distribution of Tana Ware pottery—named after the original site in Kenya, with its characteristic triangular incised decoration—to coastal, hinterland, and island settlements complements the language evidence for the migration of proto-Swahili.

How does this historical process, covering a vast part of the western Indian Ocean littoral and its offshore islands, relate to the peopling of Madagascar by Austronesian-speaking people? The basic historical problem is that although Madagascar is an African island, its people speak an Austronesian language, Malagasy, that is part of the Western Malayo-Polynesian subfamily with its closest linguistic relative being Manyaan, a language spoken on the island of Borneo. Conflicting theories about when and by what route Austronesian pioneers reached and settled Madagascar have flourished since the late nineteenth century. One school of thought favors a direct open-sea route across the central Indian Ocean, another supports a passage that followed the combination of open-sea and coastal sailing that characterized Indian Ocean trading networks. Among the latter, some scholars favor a route along the East African coast and then across to the Comoros and northwest Madagascar, while others lean toward a direct sailing route from southern India to Madagascar. What is certain is that—given the maritime skills of the Austronesians and the patterns of Indian Ocean winds and currents—all these routes were possible, but there is no unambiguous evidence for any of them.

While the details are often disputed and the evidence sometimes stretched beyond recognition, there is general agreement that the initial voyages probably reached northern Madagascar sometime between around 100 BCE to 300–400 CE, while further settlement continued sporadically for another one thousand years. What we can demonstrate is that the distribution of both the double- and single-outrigger canoe follows the known trading networks of the Indian Ocean across to Sri Lanka and southern India, and then along the African coast over to the Comoros and Madagascar. There is also archaeological evidence from first-century BCE Zanzibar that chickens had been introduced from Southeast Asia. Against this there is absolutely no evidence of Austronesian influence on Swahili or any of the modern Bantu languages of the Mozambique coast that faces western Madagascar. Even the facts that the modern population of Madagascar incorporates a significant proportion of people of African ancestry and that Malagasy includes many words of Bantu origin do not resolve the conundrum, since there is no question that—once populated—there were regular contacts between the people of Madagascar and those of Comoro Islands and the African coast.

Similarly, unresolved questions about the routing and dating of the dissemination to Africa of Southeast Asian food crops like the banana (*Musa x paradisiacal*), the water yam (*Dioscorea alata*), and the taro or cocoyam (*Colocasia esculenta*) cannot resolve this question. However, at least one proto–Northeast Bantu (ca. 300–500 CE) term for *Musa* derives from an ancestral form of Malagasy, which implies a direct Austronesian introduction of this important food crop. It is worth noting, however, that remains of coconut (*Cocos nucifera*), the fruit of a tree of probably Southeast Asian origin, have been found at Berenike, adding to the incidental evidence favoring the monsoonal trading networks of the Indian Ocean. In the end, what can be said is that at about the same time as the proto-Swahili were expanding down the African coast and onto its offshore islands, proto-Malagasy, quite probably following all the routes noted above at various moments in time and venturing in small groups of both men and women, the ultimate transmitters of their Malayo-Polynesian mother tongue, were at the beginning stages of settling the part of Madagascar nearest to this region of Bantu expansion. Most likely connections between African speakers of Bantu languages and Malagasy initially developed in fits and starts, but over time their destinies as Indian Ocean peoples became more intimately connected through trade to produce the Afrasian culture today known as Malagasy.

The initial centuries of the Current Era were marked politically by the emergence of expansive new states such as the Sassanians in Persia, the Guptas in India, and Funan in Southeast Asia around the continental rims of the Indian Ocean that both attempted to control trade and emphasized the importance of the sea route for trade. Together with the opening of direct open-sea routes across both halves of the Indian Ocean, these land-based developments stimulated the exchange of goods, people, and ideas across the entire region. In the mid-sixth century, however, Indian Ocean trade experienced a precipitous decline that paralleled the decline of these major states. Although historians remain uncertain of why this crisis occurred, one possible explanation may be the almost global epidemic of bubonic plague that swept the Old World in the mid-sixth century, known to historians of the ancient world as the Plague of Justinian. Plague is a disease carried by fleas that infested the now widespread species of Indian black rat that probably traveled uninvited aboard Indian Ocean ships. It is indeed ironic that the spread of this dread disease may have been a consequence of the very integration of the Indian Ocean world.

Recovery from the collapse of the Indian Ocean trading network took decades to achieve. A century later, however, developments at both ends of the Indian Ocean world combined to stimulate a new age of vigorous exchange that gave rise to an even more robust system of both commercial and cultural exchange across its waters and around its shores.

CHAPTER 3

Becoming an Islamic Sea

In 878, rebel forces opposed to the imperial Chinese regime massacred the Arab and Persian merchants who had come by then to dominate China's overseas trade at the inland Pearl River port of Guangzhou. According to the account written in 920 by Abu Zaid Hasan, from the Persian port of Siraf:

> They [the rebels] raised their hands to oppress the foreign merchants who had come to their country; and to these events was joined the rise of oppression and transgression in the treatment of the Arab ship-masters and captains. They imposed illegal burdens on the merchants and appropriated their wealth, and made lawful for themselves what had not been practiced formerly in any of their dealings. Wherefore God Almighty removed every blessing from them and the sea became inaccessible to them, and by the power of the blessed Creator who governs the world disaster reached [even] the captains and pilots in Sīrāf and ʿUmān.[1]

While Abu Zaid's account records the closure to a major period of extensive direct seaborne trade from the Gulf to China, this singular moment of violence captures the extraordinary growth of Indian Ocean commerce over a few short centuries following the parallel rise of Islam in Arabia from 622 and the emergence of the Tang dynasty in China in 618.

From its beginnings as a land-based religious and social revolution in the Hejaz region of Arabia, the rapid expansion of Islam very quickly registered a major transformation across the western Indian Ocean world. Following the submission of the Arabian Peninsula during the lifetime of the Prophet Muhammad, the conquest of Egypt to the west and of Persia to the east within three decades of his death in 632 suddenly established Islam as the dominant faith of the Red Sea, the Gulf, and the Arabian Sea coasts. Under the Umayyad Caliphate by the middle of the eighth century Islam had spread east to beyond the Indus River delta, while merchants from the Islamic world of the Gulf had begun to explore Indian Ocean markets down the coasts of eastern Africa and western India.

Under the Abbasid dynasty, which ruled from Baghdad from 750 to 1258, a new era of political stability—an essential factor for commercial prosperity—dominated the western Indian Ocean world, although it was challenged on its western frontier by the Shia Fatimid Caliphate, which ruled Egypt from 909 to 1171 from Fustat or Old Cairo and pacified the Red Sea route linking the Mediterranean world to that of the Indian Ocean. At the same time the demand grew for luxury goods at the center of the caliphate, driving Muslim merchants farther out into the Indian Ocean world to secure these items through trade. Over time Arabic, the language of Islam, became the lingua franca of western Indian Ocean trade, while Islamic law provided a legal framework for regulating trade.

To the east, the rise of the Tang dynasty, whose emperors ruled China from 618 to 907, effected a similar period of political stability and economic prosperity that marked a high point for the Nanhai or South China trade. Following a period of civil war in the first half of the tenth century, imperial consolidation under the Northern Sung (960–1126) and Southern Sung (1127–1279) dynasties led to increased consumer demands for luxury goods and enlarged the zone of Chinese cultural influence in a way that paralleled the rise of Islam. Together with the expansion of Islam and the energetic, outward-looking commercial activity of both Arab and Persian merchants, the political economy of imperial China contributed to the development of a single Indian Ocean trading circuit that endured to about 1000 CE.

The early decades of the Tang dynasty featured the establishment of direct trade by Persian merchants with China. Although numbers are inexact, there was a large community of Muslim merchants at Guangzhou that may have numbered in the thousands. Like many stranger communities around the world before the modern era, they were essentially internally self-governing. They built their own mosques, had their own *qadi*, or Islamic jurist, and governed themselves through Islamic institutions. Building of the Huaisheng Mosque, also known as the Lighthouse Mosque because it was used as a beacon by ships entering the port of Guangzhou, was attributed to an uncle of the Prophet Muhammad in the middle of the seventh century CE. Even if this story is more myth than history, there is no doubt that there was a flourishing Muslim community at Guangzhou and in other major South China commercial centers at a very early moment in the history of the faith.

Official missions from both mainland and island Southeast Asia, as well as from India, flocked to a peaceful and prosperous South China in the middle decades of the seventh century. How did the Chinese seek to

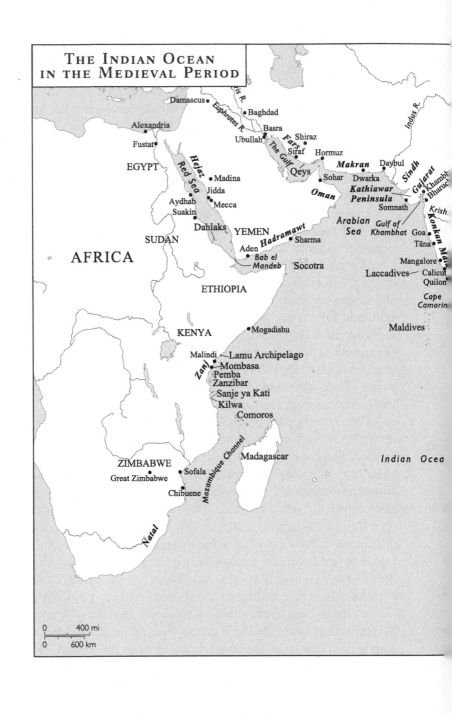

THE INDIAN OCEAN
IN THE MEDIEVAL PERIOD

Damascus
Tigris R.
Euphrates R.
Baghdad
Basra
Ubullah
The Gulf
Shiraz
Fars
Siraf
Hormuz
Indus R.
Alexandria
Fustat
Hejaz
Red Sea
Madina
Jidda
Mecca
Aydhab
Suakin
Dahlaks
Qeys
Makran
Daybul
Sindh
Sohar
Dwarka
Gujarat
Khambh.
Bharuch
EGYPT
Oman
Kathiawar
Peninsula
Somnath
Krishn.
SUDAN
YEMEN
Hadramawt
Arabian
Sea
Gulf of
Khambhat
Goa
Konkan Ma...
Tāna
AFRICA
Aden
Sharma
Mangalore
Bab el
Mandeb
Socotra
Laccadives
Calicut
Quilon
ETHIOPIA
Cape
Camorin
Maldives
KENYA
Mogadishu
Malindi
Lamu Archipelago
Zanj
Mombasa
Pemba
Zanzibar
Sanje ya Kati
Kilwa
Comoros
ZIMBABWE
Madagascar
Indian Ocea
Great Zimbabwe
Sofala
Mozambique Channel
Chibuene
Natal

0   400 mi
0   600 km

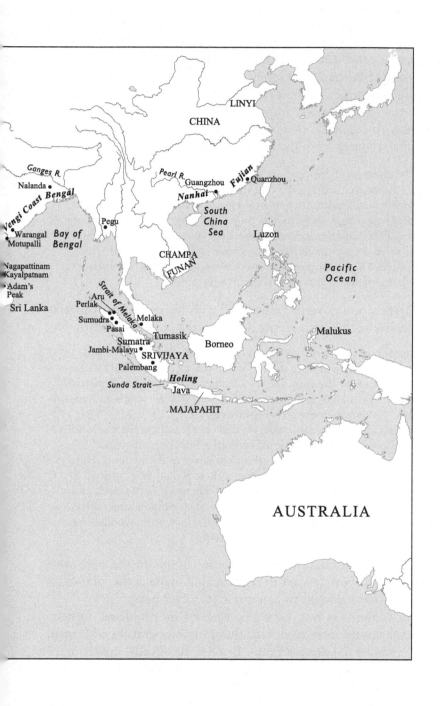

CHINA

LINYI

Ganges R.

Nalanda ●

Vengi Coast Bengal

Pearl R.

Guangzhou ● ● Quanzhou

Fujian

Nanhai

Pegu ●

Warangal Bay of
Motupalli Bengal

South
China
Sea

Luzon

Nagapattinam
Kayalpatnam

Adam's
Peak

Sri Lanka

CHAMPA

FUNAN

Pacific
Ocean

Strait of Melaka

Aru

Perlak

Sumudra ●

Pasai

Sumatra

Jambi-Malayu ●

Palembang ●

Sunda Strait

Melaka ●

Tumasik

Borneo

Malukus

SRIVIJAYA

Holing

Java

MAJAPAHIT

AUSTRALIA

deal with this important influx of, first, Kunlun Malay merchants and, later, Persian and Arab merchants? Sometime before 714 the central imperial government created the post of Superintendent of the Shipping Trade, which in other Chinese records of the period is referred to as Superintendent of Barbarian Shipping, a title that reveals more about imperial Chinese attitudes than it does about Southeast Asian societies. The reason to create this new imperial post was to regulate the trade with the southern oceans, known in China as the Nanhai trade. According to an official source from the beginning of the ninth century,

> When [the laden Nanhai ships] arrive, a report is sent to the Court and announcements are made to the cities. The captains who commanded them [or chief merchants] are made to register with the Superintendant of the Shipping Trade their names and their cargo [or submit their manifests]. [The Superintendant] collects the duties on the goods and sees that there are no [prohibited] precious and rare goods [of which the government had a monopoly]. There were some foreign merchants who were imprisoned for trying to deceive [him].[2]

Occasionally, the local governor interfered with the role of the superintendent, as is recorded in this report dating to the period 817–20:

> When the foreign ships arrive and are docking, they are charged a lowering-anchor-tax [tonnage dues]. [When the cargo is landed], there is an examination of the merchandise. Rhinoceros [horns] and pearls were so numerous that bribes were offered to the servants and retainers: the Governor stopped this [practice].
>
> Far across the seas in the South, there were those [merchants] who died in the countries there. The officials [the Superintendant and his subordinates?] held their goods. And if their wives or their sons did not come within three months to claim them, these would be confiscated. The governor [stopping this practice] said, "The sea journey back and forth is calculated in years; why fix the time in months. If anyone has proof [of his relationship with a dead man], no matter whether he comes early or late, let him have all [the goods]."[3]

These practices and thoughtful actions bear witness to the care with which the Chinese court wished to regulate and manage the vital overseas commerce that it sought to contain in its major ports.

Trade in China was not, however, without its problems. Official corruption sometimes interfered with the smooth operation of foreign merchants' commercial transactions. In 684 the greedy governor of Guangzhou "tried to cheat them of their goods, [so] the K'un-lun [came] with daggers hidden by their bodies and killed him."[4] Following another period of good administration and prosperity, a decline in trade that caused Chinese officials to squeeze foreign merchants for excessive fees precipitated the sack of Guangzhou in 758 by both Muslim and non-Muslim merchants, who "pillaged the godowns, burnt the buildings and then escaped by sea."[5] After several decades when Persian and Arab merchants abandoned Guangzhou for other East Asian ports of trade, Guangzhou re-established itself as the center of the Nanhai trade, the beginning of the end of which dates to the cataclysmic events of 878 described above.

China was certainly the farthest destination to the east of traders from the western Indian Ocean, but the Nanhai trade itself had a long history that connected it to Southeast and South Asia. During the first century of the Tang dynasty the most important state trading partner with China was known as Linyi, an area inhabited by the Cham people of coastal Vietnam who spoke an Austronesian language and had adopted Hinduism. In the fifth century, when Funan was the dominant trading state of peninsular Southeast Asia, the coastal sojourners of this region had been regarded by the Chinese as notorious pirates. Linyi was a source for a variety of indigenous primary products like ivory, rhinoceros horn, fragrant gaharuwood, tortoise-shell, and amber, as well as articles worked in gold and silver. After the middle of the eighth century, however, this trade appears to have diminished, probably because Persian and Arab merchants preferred to sail directly to ports like Guangzhou rather than lay over in the competing ports of trade of Champa, as Linyi was now called. Elsewhere in the region China traded with ports located on the Malay Peninsula, Sumatra, Bali, and Java. Following the sack of Guangzhou in 758 it appears that many Persian and Arab merchants found a welcome at the important Javanese maritime state of Holing. By the mid-ninth century, however, although Holing maintained commercial ties to South China, its less favorable position on the open sea route to China and, therefore, in the wider Indian Ocean trade contributed to its being superseded by the Sumatran state of Srivijaya.

Founded by local Malay chiefs in 670, Srivijaya came to dominate the Strait of Melaka shores to create an unrivaled regional maritime empire that endured for three and a half centuries until its defeat by a fleet dispatched by the southeast Indian Tamil state of Chola in 1025. Srivijaya's main city of Palembang was located some 80 km upstream on a navigable river that featured a fine harbor. It also benefited from a rich agricultural hinterland. Its location in southeast Sumatra placed it midway between the Strait of Melaka and the Sunda Strait, the only two passageways between the South China Sea and the main body of the Indian Ocean. Its domination of the river-mouth ports of Sumatra and the Melaka Strait was, not surprisingly, more a matter of force than of geography. By bringing the sea-sojourners of this critical Indian Ocean choke point under their control the rulers of Srivijaya built a maritime empire more powerful than any that had preceded it.

As was customary in state-trading relations, Srivijaya's rulers sent several missions to China immediately after coming to power in the seventh century. Its dominance in the Nanhai trade into the early eighth century was such that, according to the chronicle of the Tang dynasty, its rulers "sent several missions to the [Chinese] court to submit complaints about border officials seizing [their goods], and an edict was issued ordering [the officials at] Guangzhou to appease them [by making inquiries]."[6] No doubt this kind of extortion by imperial Chinese officials is what fueled subsequent attacks by Kunlun merchants on Chinese port officials. As direct trade between merchants from the western Indian Ocean and China developed during this period, Palembang became the most important regional entrepôt in that route and was thereby able to maintain strong commercial ties to China without dispatching further state missions.

Although Funan had pioneered the Southeast Asian integration of Indian religions and statecraft, Srivijaya was most closely associated with the regional expansion of Buddhism. Yet even it was influenced by Hinduism. This process of Indianization and, especially, the regional development of Buddhism created a system of belief and an ethical framework for the exchange of goods from the Coromandel coast of southeast India across the Bay of Bengal and up to China that paralleled the impact of the expansion of Islam in the western Indian Ocean. According to the Chinese Buddhist pilgrim I Ching writing in the last quarter of the seventh century, there were one thousand priests living around Palembang. Indeed, it became a feature of the sacred geography of Buddhism during this period that pilgrims from China would spend a year or two at Palembang to prepare themselves theologically for the final voyage on to the centers of Buddhism in India. So powerful was this international connection that the Srivijayan king named Balaputradeva sent a mission to the Pala King Devpala around 860 to request permission to endow the major Buddhist monastery at Nalanda in northeast India.

Although Srivijaya remained the dominant Southeast Asian force in Indian Ocean trade during these centuries at the end of the first millennium of the Current Era, during the tenth century traders from Java had begun to carve out an independent role in the spice trade from eastern Indonesia. At the same time the new Song rulers of China sought to promote a direct connection to Java in addition to the long-standing position of Srivijaya in the Nanhai trade. As competition in insular Southeast Asia picked up, Srivijaya attacked Java unsuccessfully in 925, while in 992 the Javanese launched an attack on Srivijaya. In 1016 Srivijaya appeared to cement its domination over Java with a devastating raid that was immediately followed up by a new mission to China in 1017. The ruler of Srivijaya now called himself "king of the ocean lands."[7] But less than a decade later a Tamil inscription records that the Chola king Rajendra, "having dispatched many ships in the midst of the rolling sea," successfully carried out punitive attacks against fourteen Srivijayan ports, including Palembang.[8] So although Srivijaya remained an important factor in Indian Ocean trade for the next two centuries, its center now shifted from Palembang to the rival Sumatran port city of Jambi-Malayu. By the late twelfth century Chinese sources ranked Srivijaya third after "the realm of Ta-shih (the Arabs)" and Java in their oceanic trade relations.[9]

The path followed by traders from "the realm of Ta-shih" to Song China reflected only one aspect of the Indian Ocean expansion of Muslim traders and Islam. Once the military expansion, state building, and religious consolidation that marked the century or so following the death of the Prophet was achieved, maritime trade, Arab and Persian settlement, and the gradual growth of Islam around the coast of the western Indian Ocean followed. There was also scriptural justification for such a development. According to verse 31 of the 31st or Surah Luqman of the Holy Quran, "See you not that the ships sail through the sea by Allah's Grace? That He may show you of His Signs? Verily, in this are signs for every patient, grateful (person)."[10] Although divisions within Islam had appeared by the end of the seventh century CE and despite the political rivalries that emanated from divisions between Sunni and Shia Muslims, by and large these theological differences did not play themselves out as dramatically in the world of Indian Ocean trade as they did in the geopolitical struggles of land-based Islamic states. Rather, the growing concept of the 'umma—the community of believers—contributed to group cohesiveness at the local, regional, and transregional levels, especially where Muslims were a minority population, and in most cases did not inhibit commercial relations between members of different Muslim communities of belief. Similarly, Islamic law provided a legal framework for the business of trade within the different Muslim communities.

The seventh-century Arab invasion of Persia and political consolidation of the early caliphates not only initiated a process of conversion to Islam and Arabization, but also pushed Persian Zoroastrians, Nestorian Christians, and eventually dissident Muslims out from the Gulf into the Indian Ocean trade. Many of these adventurers established themselves in the trading emporia of western India and eastern Africa. If Indian Ocean trade was ignored in the first century of the Islamic era, the relocation of the imperial capital from Damascus to Baghdad under the Abbasids encouraged official interest in this lucrative luxury trade. Located between the Tigris and Euphrates rivers, Baghdad had easy access to the Indian Ocean through the port of Ubullah, near Basra. Under the Abbasids the major Persian ports were, from north to south, Siraf, Qeys, and Hormuz. In addition, in the Arabian ports of Aden and Jidda many inhabitants were Arabic-speaking Persians, while Persian influence was important at the Omani port of Sohar. It should be no surprise, therefore, that their religious compatriots turned up among the foreign traders in China at this time.

Situated on a narrow coastal shelf with high mountains behind it in the district named for the Sassanian king Ardasir, Siraf was unquestionably the most important of the Persian ports of trade. With deep water access, a good anchorage, and protected from the prevailing storms of the Gulf, Siraf was well located to take advantage of the ninth-century boom in Indian Ocean trade. Although its food had to be imported from the sea, its location on the direct route between the Gulf and China, plus its access by overland caravan to Shiraz, the capital of the Shia Buyid dynasty that dominated the waning Abbasid Caliphate, made it a classic nexus for the meeting of land and sea trade routes. It was also a major center for the construction of dhows, the wood for which came from eastern Africa, as did that for its houses. Indeed, an interesting aspect of western Indian Ocean material culture from this time is that the average length—no more than four meters—of East African mangrove pole rafters, called *boriti* in Swahili, used in house construction at Siraf and widely throughout the region, imposed common limitations on the dimensions of domestic architecture from the Swahili coast to the Gulf.

The tenth-century Arab traveler and geographer Ibn Hawqal keenly observed of Siraf that "the inhabitants devote their whole time to commerce and merchandise."[11] Siraf dispatched ships and merchants to the Red Sea, the East African coast and its offshore islands, western India, Sri Lanka, and on to China. Another indicator of its central place in Indian Ocean trade is the distribution of unglazed earthenwares manufactured at Siraf and glazed Sassanian-Islamic ceramics in archaeological sites to ports around the western Indian Ocean. Its exceptional wealth, which the great eleventh-century Arab geographer al-Maqdisi described as surpassing that of Basra, derived entirely from the Indian Ocean trade. He noted the beauty of its houses and gardens, as well as its place at the center of the Persia-China trade. "In the whole lands of Islam there were no more remarkable mansions than those of Siraf."[12]

A devastating earthquake in 977 marked the end of Siraf's heyday in dominating Indian Ocean trade. In the first centuries of the second millennium CE it was surpassed by Gulf rivals, Qeys, an island off the southwest coast of Iran; Hormuz, on the south coast of Iran; and Sohar, in Oman. Another major Indian Ocean transit entrepôt that was probably founded at this time by both Arab and Persian Gulf merchants was Sharma, on the coast of Hadramawt. Linking the ports of the Arabian Sea to those of the Red Sea, especially Aden, Sharma flourished from about 980 to 1140, when it was attacked from the Red Sea. It was a strongly fortified town with some eighty large buildings that were probably commercial warehouses. The abundant ceramic finds at Sharma include imports from all over the Indian Ocean world, from as far as China and Sri Lanka, to the east, and Africa, to the west. Africa also supplied Sharma with large quantities of copal resins, which were valued for use as incense. Sharma is a prime example of how a port emerged at a particular moment in Indian Ocean history in response to changes in the commercial networks linking changes in the Gulf, Red Sea, and Swahili coast. Despite the relative decline of Siraf and Shiraz, the cultural influence of the Gulf became a permanent feature of Islamic identity on the Swahili coast and its offshore islands, where claims of Shirazi forebears as a prestigious marker of social status and political leadership have endured to the present.

The earliest evidence for the expansion of Islam to coastal East Africa dates to the eighth century, when adventurous merchants from the Gulf made their way down the coast from ports like Mogadishu to Zanzibar in search of trading partners. These intrepid adventurers carried with them both luxury trade goods from the entire Indian Ocean region and the new ideas about religion and political leadership emanating from the Gulf. Physical evidence of their presence comes from shards of Chinese and Indian pottery, and large quantities of both unglazed Siraf pottery and Sassanian-Islamic ceramic wares. These were especially prominent at Manda, in the Lamu archipelago, but were also significant at Zanzibar and Kilwa. A few fragments of Sassanian-Islamic ware have also been found as far south as coastal Madagascar and Natal.

The earliest signs of Islam on the Swahili coast appear as mosques and date to the second half of the eighth century. Early tombs were small, as befit initial immigrant communities, and some were constructed of local timber, but as these pioneering communities attracted African converts and grew, so did mosques, which were now constructed in local coral rag. Shanga, in the Lamu archipelago; Ras Mkumbuu, on Pemba island; and Unguja Ukuu, on Zanzibar, feature such early mosques dating to the mid-eighth to the early eleventh centuries. Muslim burials from the same period are found at Mtambwe Mkuu, on Pemba, and at Chibuene, on the coast of southern Mozambique. Finally, the earliest Arabic inscription on the coast can be seen in the *mihrab* of the mosque at Kizimkazi at the south end of Zanzibar, which records the building of the mosque in 1107 CE. Carved in an elaborate Kufic script, the inscription suggests a possible connection to Siraf, either by importation or inspiration.

The Shirazi tradition reflects more than a specific connection to either Siraf or Shiraz, but more generally points to the greater Gulf region that dominated this foundational period of Islam on the Swahili coast. Early Islamic communities were established by mainly dissident Muslims—Shias, Ibadis, Kharajites—seeking refuge in the frontier region of the African coast. The rise of Siraf and its links to the capital of the Buyid dynasty that commanded the caliphate between 945 and 1055 established Shiism as the dominant sect linking the Gulf to the Swahili coast.

The integration of foreign Muslims into coastal East African society resulted from the intermarriage of men from the Gulf with local women, preferably from locally prominent families who could facilitate trade. As Muslims, their children would have claimed the Gulf origins of their fathers; indeed, such sons may well have traveled to the Gulf with their male relatives. Yet they would also have drawn upon the familial connections of their African mothers. Neither identity was necessarily exclusive of the other; indeed, depending on the situation, it made good sense for such individuals to be able to claim both. Over time, as some of the descendants of these Indian Ocean unions gained commercial prominence or staked claim to local political leadership, their forefathers' "Shirazi" origins became fixed into local traditions. Thus, in some places "Shirazi" *nisbas* or patronymics feature in genealogies from this early period, while ruling dynasties claiming Shirazi origins became prominent from the coast of southern Kenya right down to the Comoros. Such claims cannot be taken at face value, but they do reflect significant Gulf influence on the Indian Ocean side of Muslim town formation along the Swahili coast and its offshore islands. How different was this historical process from the experience of Arabo-Persian Muslim merchants in China at the same time!

The most important early towns of the Swahili coast were located to the north, as these provided the nearest landfall to ships sailing from the Gulf. There is archaeological evidence to suggest that some of these settlements, particularly Mtambwe Mkuu, may have been favored by Ibadi Muslims who had been pushed out of Oman by the Umayyads. As Shia Muslims from the Gulf became dominant in the northern towns, some Ibadis migrated south to the island of Sanje ya Kati, in the same protected bay as Kilwa Kisiwani, "Kilwa on the Island," on the coast of southern mainland Tanzania. Not surprisingly, the two walled towns became rivals, a struggle that probably focused on control of the seaborne gold trade with Sofala, located on the southern coast of Mozambique. By the twelfth century, however, headed by a dynasty claiming Shirazi origins, Kilwa Kisiwani had emerged as the dominant city-state on the entire coast because of its control of the gold trade.

What is remarkable about this commerce is that the gold that fueled Kilwa's economic and political dominance of the coast came from deep in the interior of south-central Africa, not from its own continental hinterland. It was mined in auriferous or gold-bearing seams on the high plateau of modern Zimbabwe and transported overland down to the central Mozambican port of Sofala. Sofala was already known as a major coastal port to Arab and Persian travelers in the early tenth century. Sometime during that century its rulers converted to Islam and probably claimed ties to the Gulf. By the mid-eleventh century control of gold production was a factor in the rise of the state whose rulers caused the construction of Great Zimbabwe. They probably also extended their domination to Sofala until the rulers of Kilwa seized control of the port in the twelfth century. Thus, the golden hinterland of Kilwa was hundreds of miles south by sea and accessible only through the port of Sofala.

When Ibn Battuta visited the Swahili coast in 1331 the ship that carried him dropped anchor at Mogadishu, Mombasa, and Kilwa. He describes Mogadishu as "an enormous town" populated by merchants who daily slaughtered hundreds of camels for food.

> When a vessel reaches the port, it is met by *sumbuqs*, which are small boats, in each of which are a number of young men, each carrying a covered dish containing food. He presents this to one of the merchants on the ship saying "this is my guest," and all the others do the same. Each merchant on disembarking goes only to the house of the young man who is his host, except those who have made frequent journeys to the town and know its people well; these live where they please. The

host then sells his goods for him and buys for him, and if anyone buys anything from him at too low a price or sells to him in the absence of his host, the sale is regarded by them as invalid.[13]

Ibn Battuta's account reflects the fact that Mogadishu was an open roadstead and that ocean-going ships had to be served by local lighters to offload and load their passengers and trade goods. The trading system he describes was a well-developed mechanism by which a stranger-merchant was represented by a host, called in Somali *abban*. In most cases, one's original abban would continue to serve as a merchant's host on future trips, something that the Moroccan visitor seems not to have recognized. Such a system would also have served as a means to integrate outsiders into the local community of Mogadishu.

As he was a learned man and not a merchant, the town qadi served as host to Ibn Battuta, but not before visiting the local sultan, who spoke both "the Maqdishi language," which by that time would have been Somali, and Arabic. At his reception Ibn Battuta was offered "a plate containing betel leaves and areca nuts,"[14] the basic components of *paan*, a sign of South Asian hospitality that belies a clear Indian Ocean influence. Three days later he embarked for Kilwa after worshipping at the local mosque with the sultan.

Ibn Battuta spent only a single night at the island town of Mombasa, whose inhabitants he described as "pious, honourable, and upright." At Kilwa he noted that "the majority of its inhabitants are Zanj, jet-black in colour, and with tattoo-marks on their faces." He learned that Sofala was located a fortnight away to the south and that the source of gold was a month's journey inland. The ruler of Kilwa during his visit, Hasan b. Sulaiman, "was noted for his gifts and generosity" in accordance with the prescriptions of the Quran.[15] This ruler did not, however, claim Shirazi origins. Rather, he was the scion of a new dynasty with family origins in Yemen, the Mahdali, that had seized power at Kilwa in about 1280. As direct descendants from the Prophet Muhammad, the Mahdali enjoyed a form of religious charisma or blessedness called *baraka* that endowed them with a special place within Sunni Muslim society. For Ibn Battuta the Swahili coast towns he visited represented mainstream Sunni Islam. In a word, no later than the early fourteenth century the Ibadi and Shia Islam of the Gulf had been largely replaced by the Sunni Shafii rite that was espoused by the Arabian heartland and had become the majority tendency in world Islam.

If African gold and ivory, not to forget timber, were the principal attractions for Indian Ocean traders, bonded labor was another. Early in the history of the Abbasid Caliphate its rulers determined to drain the saline marshes of southern Iraq to be able to convert the land to agriculture. To do so was a prodigious task requiring large inputs of human labor. To meet these new labor requirements the Abbasid rulers caused a great increase in the slave trade from eastern Africa, including both northeast Africa and the Swahili coast. Enslaved Africans from the Sudan and Ethiopia were shipped from Red Sea ports directly to Basra or indirectly through Arabia, where they were transported overland to southern Iraq. Those from farther south were embarked from different towns on the Swahili or Zanj coast, as it was also known to the Arabs. By the middle decades of the ninth century conditions of work in the marshes were so intolerable that the enslaved workers rose up in revolt in what is known as the Zanj Revolt.

Enslaved Africans were already familiar in the Middle East and claimed an important role in the early history of Islam. One of the Prophet's earliest companions and the first *muezzin* or caller to prayers of the new faith was the emancipated African Bilal b. Rabah al-Habashi, this last name indicating he was from Ethiopia. The scale of slavery was greatly increased, however, during the state-building of subsequent centuries. The Abbasid Caliphs employed thousands of domestic slaves and slave soldiers, among them so-called Zanj slaves to designate their origins from coastal eastern Africa. Before the Zanj Revolt proper, the project of resuscitating the agricultural lands of southern Iraq produced small slave uprisings in 689–90, 694, and 760. When the great revolt began a century later it created havoc for the Abbasid dynasty.

Despite its designation as the Zanj Revolt, this social movement against Abbasid exploitation involved free and enslaved Africans from both northeast and East Africa, while its leader was a free Arab whose grandmother was an Indian concubine. Embracing the radical egalitarianism of Kharijite Islam, the revolt lasted from 869 into 883, recruiting broad support from among all the lower classes in southern Iraq. Flush with a series of early successes, the movement's leadership quickly formed an independent state that seized control of the southern reaches of the caliphate, including the key Indian Ocean port cities of Ubullah and Basra. A combination of armed force and the offer of amnesty eventually caused the collapse of the Zanj state, driving many of its fighters, both Arab and African, into exile. The Zanj Revolt convinced the Abbasid ruling classes that the concentration of bonded agricultural labor was not a good idea, so while slavery as an institution certainly continued to exist in the caliphate, the extreme demand for enslaved labor from Africa to supply it that characterized this era was not to be replicated until the late eighteenth and nineteenth centuries.

A century later, according to Buzurg b. Shahriyar, a Persian *nakhuda* or merchant shipowner who probably sailed out of Hormuz, the Swahili coast was attacked by a massive fleet from Madagascar. Buzurg recounted that "they came with a thousand small boats and violently attacked the town of Qanbalu," most probably Ras Mkumbuu on Pemba, both to obtain trade goods "useful in their country and for China . . . and because they wanted to obtain Zanj, for they were strong and easily endured slavery." The history of the Zanj Revolt suggests otherwise, but this account stands as evidence that the Malagasy may have continued to augment their diverse population by periodic slave raids on the coast. In the same passage, Buzurg adds, "They said their voyage lasted a year. They had pillaged some islands six days away, and then several villages and towns belonging to Sofala in the land of the Zanj."[16] Although Buzurg is not always the most reliable author, his testimony anticipates equally massive and devastating maritime slave raids launched by Malagasy in outrigger canoes on the Comoros and Swahili coast in the late eighteenth and early nineteenth centuries.

If the Gulf dominated the commercial history of the western Indian Ocean during these centuries, the Red Sea also experienced a revival of its fortunes after the rise of Islam. The critical factor in this process was the coming to power of the Fatimids, a Shia Ismaili dynasty based at Fustat, or Old Cairo, who ruled Egypt from 969 to 1171. Conflict with Christian powers in the Mediterranean turned the Fatimids toward the Indian Ocean and emphasized the importance of Aden as the critical entrepôt between the Indian Ocean and the Red Sea. Protected from the Arabian hinterland by a precipitous caldera of volcanic mountains, Aden was an isolated peninsula close to the strategic choke point of the Bab el Mandeb that enjoyed an excellent anchorage. As many as fifteen ships could anchor in its harbor where lighters would ferry goods to and from the city's customs house. Contemporary Jewish correspondence relating to the India trade retrieved from the medieval Cairo Geniza, a repository for any paper with the name of God on it, states that Aden played host to "ships from every sea," including "ships from India and its environs, ships from the land of Zanj and environs, ships from Berbera and Habash and environs, ships from al-Ashār and al-Qamr and environs,"[17] that is, the coasts of northeast Africa and southern Arabia where the port of Sharma was located. At Aden one could see different types of ships from the Indian Ocean world, as well as Arab, Persian, Jewish, Indian, and Ethiopian nakhudas. The town itself combined stone buildings for the elites, fortifications to protect it from seaside or mainland attack, and more humble and numerous palm-frond huts.

At Aden, business interests trumped any and all potential communal divisions. While ethnic and religious communities managed their own affairs internally, when matters crossed these boundaries the city authorities adjudicated a solution. Although there was undoubtedly competition for business, and while commercial affairs were largely constructed within bounded communities, some cross-cultural partnerships also formed. A notable case involved the Jewish nakhuda Mahruz and his Indian counterpart Tinbu. In a letter to his brother-in-law, whose ship was attacked by pirates along the Konkan coast of western India so that he was forced to take refuge in the Gujarati port of Bharuch, Mahruz urged his relative to contact Tinbu if he needed money for the trip back to Aden. "If my lord, you need any gold, please take it on my account from the nākhodā Tinbū, for he is staying in Tāna [on the Konkan coast], and between him and me there are strong bonds of inseparable friendship and brotherhood."[18]

Not surprisingly, Aden's success attracted the cupidity of its Indian Ocean rivals. In 1134–35 a naval force from Qeys laid siege to Aden that took many months to break and disperse. Ships plying the Red Sea also had to deal with rivals based at the Dahlak Islands, off the coast of Eritrea. Whether they were subject to high—possibly extortionate—tariffs levied by the local rulers of the Dahlaks or whether they claimed to be threatened by pirates from the Dahlaks, it appears that the western side of the lower Red Sea was a difficult place for merchants traveling between Egypt and India. A different consequence of the increased significance of the Red Sea trade and the decline of the Gulf was that the seaborne route to India came to emphasize the ports of the Konkan and Malabar coastline of southwestern India to the disadvantage of those of Gujarat and Sindh.

In 1173 the Ayyubids seized Aden and were eager to maintain it as the emporium for collecting revenue from the India trade. Although Aden continued to flourish under the Ayyubids, within half a century they were replaced by the Rasulid dynasty of Yemen, which ruled over all of south Arabia from 1229 to 1454. By incorporating Aden into a unified southern Yemeni state the Rasulids actually enhanced the commercial position of Aden, which now also served as an outlet for the trade in Arabian horses, which were highly sought after by the rulers of the major states of southern India. Aden alone produced one-third of the state revenue for the Rasulids by enabling them to control the India-Egypt trade. The Rasulid navy escorted as many as one hundred ships plying the Red Sea route linking Cairo to Aden, while all vessels sailing from India to the Red Sea were required to pass through the customs house at Aden.

In 1420 or 1421, however, an especially greedy Rasulid sultan extorted all the silk and spices brought to Aden from India. Facing financial ruin, the nakhudas sought to break this monopoly. In the following two years a Muslim Indian merchant shipowner named Ibrahim from Calicut, the most important transit entrepôt on the Malabar coast, tried unsuccessfully to circumvent Aden, once by sailing directly to Jidda, the main port of the Hejaz, then by heading to the Dahlak Islands. At last, in 1424 Ibrahim was able to bring three ships to Jidda, where a special envoy sent there by the Mamluk sultan of Egypt, Barsbay, enabled him to disembark and sell his goods in security. The next year fourteen Indian vessels followed suit and in 1426 the number rose to forty. In the blink of an eye the seasonal port of Jidda, which had previously only come to life during the annual pilgrimage to Mecca and Medina, had replaced Aden as the main port for the India trade. This radical shift reflected the combined power wielded by the merchant shipowners who financed this Indian Ocean trade.

If by the fourteenth century Islam had become the dominant faith around the western coast of the Indian Ocean, its proselytizing success was both slower and less complete in South and Southeast Asia. Although Islam had reached Sindh in the second decade of the eighth century CE, it remained an isolated outlier until the Turkic conquest of northern India began at the end of the tenth century. Under the Hindu dynasty of the Caulukyas (941–1297), Gujarat remained outside the Muslim sphere. Although their center of power was in northern Gujarat, the Caulukyas promoted Indian Ocean trade though ports it controlled on the Gulf of Khambhat. Chief among these was Khambhat itself, the successor to Barygaza/Bharuch on the same bay.

Khambhat faced the same geographical challenges as faced Barygaza, namely dangerous fast tides, inaccessibility by sea at low tides, sand bars, and silting up. Its great advantage commercially was its immediate access to the major centers of Indian textile manufacture for the Indian Ocean trade. Under the Caulukyas it became the principal intermediary port of trade for the Aden-Melaka exchange. Its imports included precious and base metals, silk, gems, ivory, spices, wine, frankincense, and horses; its exports included textiles, dyes such as indigo, spices, aromatics, precious and semi-precious stones, and slaves. Much of this commerce was transit trade, with the same goods entering and leaving port without being distributed inland. Over time, bulk goods became more important, as did money.

The most prominent merchants of Gujarat were Jains, members of a universal faith with syncretic elements incorporated from Hinduism and Buddhism. Jains also occupied key administrative positions within the Caulukya kingdom. Jains dominated banking, credit, and continental trade, but they limited their maritime energies to coasting trade, leaving the Indian Ocean–side trade to Muslims, for whom they served as major financiers.

Muslim Arab and Persian trading settlements dotted coastal western India as far back as the eighth century. The Caulukya king Siddharaja (1094–1143) favored the Muslim traders, who gradually converted some Indians and settled in hinterland towns, including the capital city. In frequent acts of economic self-interest, Caulukya rulers often endowed mosques, as did the prominent Jain merchant-administrator at Khambhat, Vastupal (1169–1240), who was also known for his success in curbing piracy and providing security to merchants who frequented the town. Whatever their internal doctrinal differences, these Muslim trading groups generally expressed group solidarity with respect to the non-Muslim societies in which they operated. Mosque inscriptions and Muslim graves from the thirteenth century indicate that most Muslim traders were also shipowners.

Gujarat was conquered by the Muslim Delhi sultanate in 1303 and became an independent sultanate after the sack of Delhi in 1398, thereby becoming a Sunni Muslim polity. Khambhat retained its centrality as the principal Indian Ocean port of northwest India for the next two centuries, as visitors from Marco Polo to Ibn Battuta to the fifteenth-century Venetian merchant Nicolo de Conti testify. By this time, however, several ports of the Malabar coast, notably Mangalore, Calicut, Cranagore, Cochin or Kochi, and Quilon or Kollam had emerged as rivals to Khambhat as entrepôts for the trade between eastern and western Indian Oceans.

The entire coast of western India had long experienced vibrant coasting trade, particularly linking the excellent small ports of the more northerly Konkan coast. According to court poetry and inscriptions from the tenth and eleventh centuries, there was also an important maritime pilgrim's route linking various Konkan ports to Somnath, on the south Gujarat coast, where there is a temple dedicated to the God Siva. Somnath was also a renowned port. Writing in 1030, the distinguished Persian scholar al-Biruni explained, "The reason why in particular Somnath has become so famous is that it was a harbour of sea-faring people, and a station for those who went to and fro between Sufala in Zanz and China."[19] An exceptional bilingual inscription in Sanskrit and Arabic dated to 1287 records the construction of a mosque at Somnath by a nakhuda from Hormuz named Nuruddin Firuz, who is praised in the Arabic version as "the great and respected chief, prince among seamen, king of kings of merchants."[20] No less remarkable, to acquire the land on which to build the mosque Nuruddin relied upon the support of local prominent Hindu religious leaders. The entire process was then approved by the town council and ruling authorities up to the Hindu ruler of Gujarat. A different example of mosque construction in Hindu India comes from an inscription recounting the shipwreck near Goa of a Kadamba royal pilgrim who was rescued by a Muslim Arab merchant shipowner named Ali. In gratitude Ali's grandson was appointed administrator of the Goa region by Kadamba king Jayakesi. The grandson built a mosque at Goa that was to be maintained by tolls levied at that Konkani port. Distress at sea clearly also featured in the account of the Jewish merchant Mahruz reaching out to the Hindu nakhuda Tinbu.

Isolated Persian and Arab traders had certainly visited the coast of southwestern India and Sri Lanka from the early decades of the rise of Islam. As the Gulf lost its dominance of Indian Ocean trade to the Red Sea, however, Arab merchants from Arabia obtained an increasing foothold in Malabari ports. In particular, immigration from Hadramawt beginning in the thirteenth century gave a particular character to this process of settlement. In addition to the Hadrami role as traders, these intrepid maritime merchants also carried their faith, the same Sunni Shafii Islam that increasingly provided a religious nexus and legal framework for trade around the entire western Indian Ocean coast. From their port bases in peninsular India they soon moved out to proselytize the two extensive archipelagos of small islands to the southwest of India, the Laccadives and the Maldives.

Muslim traders on the Malabar coast were distinguished as either "Pardeshis," meaning "foreigners," or "Mappilas," the social product of Arabs who had married into and converted lower-caste Hindu Malabaris, mainly from groups associated with the sea. The Mappilas wore local dress, spoke the local language of Malayalam, and sometimes adopted a dual descent system to reflect the patrilineality of their Arab forebears and the matrilineal system of their mothers' kin. In many respects the integration of these Muslim Arab outsiders into South Asian society mirrors that of foreign Muslims in the towns of the Swahili coast, the main difference being that the Mappilas remained a religious minority community whereas Islam became the dominant faith and a defining part of being Swahili.

Like Muslim merchants in Hindu Gujarat, those of the Malabar coast experienced close economic and political relations with their

Hindu hosts. At Calicut, Muslim merchants enjoyed the patronage of a king called the Zamorin by foreign writers, but whose indigenous title was Samudri Raja, or "Ocean King." Muslims held office as harbor masters and, as elsewhere in the Indian Ocean world, managed their own community affairs internally through their own royally appointed "chiefs." Yet, both because of their insistence on maintaining their distinctive foreign origins as a hallmark of their identity, even distinguishing themselves from other Indian Muslims, and as a consequence of the increasingly strict caste segregation of Brahmanic Hinduism, there was a very real level of tension and conflict between Muslims and Hindus in Calicut and the other ports of southern India. Similarly, a literary biography of the rich Gujarati Hindu merchant Jagadu memorializes his rivalry over possession of a precious stone with a Muslim merchant from Hormuz who is described as an impure outsider. So while the mutual interests of business ruled to mediate relations between Hindu rulers and Muslim merchants in both Gujarat and the coastal ports of western India, as well as between different communities of nakhudas, there were also unsurprising elements of communal competition in the medieval Indian Ocean world.

Of all the Malabar coast ports Calicut was by all measures dominant. In the thirteenth century it surpassed Khambhat as the most important port of trade linking Egypt to the East. Writing in the following century, Ibn Battuta commented that it possessed "one of the largest harbours in the world. It is visited by men from China, Sumatra, Ceylon, the Maldives, Yemen and Fárs, and in it gather merchants from all quarters."[21] During his three-month visit to Calicut he counted thirteen Chinese vessels waiting for the Southwest Monsoon winds to carry them back to China. Upon their departure one of the Chinese ships was wrecked in a storm and driven ashore. This unfortunate event revealed to Ibn Battuta one reason why Calicut had become a favored port for Indian Ocean merchants. Shipwrecks everywhere attracted scavengers, but at Calicut he witnessed the Zamorin's "police officers were beating the people to prevent them from plundering what the sea cast up." Ibn Battuta goes on to explain: "In all the lands of Mulaybár, except in this one land alone, it is the custom that whenever a ship is wrecked all that is taken from it belongs to the treasury. At Cálicút however it is retained by its owners and for that reason Cálicút has become a flourishing city and attracts large numbers of merchants."[22]

Enforcing this policy regarding scavenging was not, however, unique to Calicut. A century earlier on the eastern side of the Indian Peninsula the Kakatiya ruler of Warangal, Ganapati, proclaimed a charter of security for the port of Motupalli on the Vengi coast of Andhra Pradesh at the Krishna River delta.

> By the glorious Maharaja Ganapatideva the following edict (assuring) safety has been granted to traders by sea, starting for and arriving from all continents, islands, foreign countries and cities. . . . Formerly kings used to take away by force the whole cargo, viz., gold, elephants, horses, gems, etc., carried by ships and vessels which after they had started from one country or other, were attacked by storms, wrecked and thrown on the shore.[23]

Like the protection afforded to foreign merchants in all the major trading ports of the Indian Ocean world, the prospect of security was essential to conducting business that would profit all participants.

As early as the eighth century Arab merchants also pushed beyond Cape Comorin to Sri Lanka and the Coromandel coast of southeastern India. Small port towns offered respite to merchant vessels from Southeast Asia and China on the route to Quilon and more northerly ports of Malabar. Sri Lanka was also an important pilgrimage site for Muslims because of Adam's Peak, the spot where Adam is alleged to have remained for two centuries after his banishment from the Garden of Eden. Contemporary to the great period of Chola state expansion, Muslim presence on the Coromandel coast increased notably in the eleventh century. Chola kings encouraged Tamil merchant guilds like the Manigramam and Ayyavole to expand their business to the east and created conditions for a port like Nagapattinam to develop as a major player in the trade of the eastern Indian Ocean. Srivijayan, Muslim, Jewish, and Chinese maritime merchants all gained a footing at Nagapattinam. In this latter respect the Chola acted in much the same way as the Zamorin of Calicut and the Caulukya ruler of Gujarat.

As along the Malabar coast, on the Coromandel coast Arabs continued to emphasize their Arabness and followed the Shafii school of law. Although they came to speak Tamil, they were known locally as *Ilappai* or Labbai, itself perhaps a rendering of *arabi*, and maintained their distinction from those Hanafi Muslims who adhered to a different legal tradition and who were from northern India and settled in Tamil Nadu. Notably mobile, the Labbai became known as dealers in pearls, which were obtained off Sri Lanka, and expanded their activities to Southeast Asia. Consequently, Muslim traders from ports like Kayalpatnam, on the far southeastern coast, preferred to marry women from similar communities in Sri Lanka and Indonesia, rather than from Tamil society. Their expansion was marked by the erection of mosques and

Islamic schools, as well as the development of a Tamil-Arabic dialect for worship and even scholarship, such that "Labbai" became a generic name for Muslim jewelers and merchants in the larger Malay world. Compared to Arab Muslims on India's western coast, then, those who established communities east of the subcontinent's tip chose to distinguish themselves as outsiders in Hindu lands.

The Indian Ocean world of Southeast Asia remained the religious domain of Hinduism and Buddhism until the arrival of Islam. While scattered pockets of Muslim merchants had previously operated in insular Southeast Asia, Islam began to take root only in the thirteenth century, by which time Srivijaya's regional domination of international commerce was in decline. The first small states to convert to Islam were the ports of Perlak and Aru, on the northeast coast of Sumatra, but the dominant Islamic polity to emerge in this strategically placed region for Indian Ocean trade was nearby Pasai. Like Srivijaya before it, Pasai joined downriver and upriver communities, commanding both the Melaka Strait from the port of Pasai and the pepper production of the rich agricultural lands of the interior. According to its royal chronicle, the *Hikayat Raja-Raja Pasai*, the first ruler to convert to Islam received the faith directly from Mecca and, in a dream, from the Prophet.

> Once upon a time, in the days when the Prophet Muhammad the Apostle . . . was still alive, he said to the elect of Mecca, "In time to come, when I have passed away, there will rise on the east a city called Semudera. When you hear tell of this city make ready a ship to take to it all the regalia and panoply of royalty. Guide its people into the religion of Islam. Let them recite the words of the profession of faith. For in that city shall God . . . raise up saints in great number."[24]

Although this foundational legend cannot be taken literally, it does indicate that Islam was introduced from Arabia. In addition, among Arabian merchants plying the Indian Ocean trading networks, the adherence to Sufism, a practice that emphasizes the personal and mystical dimensions of belief, proved important in conversion to Islam in Indonesia, enabling the incorporation of previous religious traditions into popular Islamic practice. Above all, what Islam offered was a new source of ritual prestige by which the rulers of Pasai could distinguish their regime from that of their Indonesian rivals.

A vivid indicator of the regional and Indian Ocean linkages forged by Islamic Pasai is a story about the fourteenth-century son of Sultan Ahmed II. "If he dressed in a Javanese costume he looked like a man of

Java. If he dressed in [Thai] costume he looked like a man of the [Thai] state. If he wore the costume of India he looked like a man of India. If he wore the costume of Arabia, like an Arab."[25]

In many respects, Pasai regarded the Javanese Buddhist kingdom of Majapahit as a model. The rise of Majapahit in 1293 marked a decided shift eastward of Southeast Asian maritime trade. It was built on control and expansion of the spice trade of the Maluku Islands, which it managed to maintain to about 1500 despite internal rivalries and the gradual Islamization of Java's northern coast in the fifteenth century.

The major regional development in the fifteenth century with respect to Indian Ocean commerce was the rise of Melaka, located on the western coast of the Malayan Peninsula. Melaka was founded by a dissident Malay prince named Paramesvara who was a vassal of Majapahit at Palembang and sought greater independence by moving with his followers to Tumasik (modern Singapore) in about 1390. Siamese pressure forced Paramesvara west to Melaka, where he organized the local Malays and forged an important alliance with imperial China. He sent envoys to China to seek its protection and visited China himself in 1411. The Chinese Muslim eunuch admiral Zheng He visited Melaka on several occasions between 1409 and the early 1430s; but when the Ming dynasty turned inward, the ruler of Melaka converted to Islam to encourage the Muslim merchants who controlled the western Indian Ocean trade to make Melaka their headquarters. Commercially motivated diplomacy was also reflected in marriages to a Tamil princess by the third ruler of Melaka and by the fifth ruler to the royal house of Majapahit. At the height of its power Melaka controlled the entire Malay Peninsula and the opposing coast of Sumatra.

Melaka became the dominant and wealthiest international entrepôt for goods in and through Southeast Asia, establishing especially close ties with Gujarati and Tamil merchants. While the Gujaratis at Melaka actually included Muslim merchants from Sri Lanka and all of western India, the Tamils were dominated by Hindu Keling traders. Muslim traders from Java who controlled the spice trade of the Malukus were another prominent community of foreigners at Melaka. All foreign traders at Melaka occupied assigned neighborhoods and each such community had its own "chief of port." The largest group of foreign merchants at Melaka were actually Chinese, a cluster that included traders from mainland Southeast Asia, among them many Muslims. Smaller foreign communities, many of whom provided artisanal and other services, included Bengalis, Peguans from Myanmar, and smaller groups of Armenians, Nestorian Christians, Jews, Yemenis, Persians, and even a mixed Muslim Filipino-Chinese community from Luzon that lived outside of Melaka. In short, Melaka was an unusually cosmopolitan international trading port, even by historic Indian Ocean standards.

Perhaps the most remarkable single phenomenon of the fifteenth century was the short period of Ming voyages into the Indian Ocean. Direct Chinese trade out into the Indian Ocean dated only to the tenth century when the Sung dynasty moved to rationalize trade by creating a partial monopoly, thereby limiting the role of foreign merchants and hoping to avoid the problems that afflicted Guangzhou in the previous century. As more ports emerged on the South China coast to take up the slack, Chinese knowledge of Indian Ocean trade increased significantly. The writings of Chou Ku-fei (1178) identify southern Arabia, the Gulf, and Southeast Asia as the main centers of desirable goods. Fifty years later, an unidentified author named Chau Ja-kua, who was called Superintendent of Maritime Trade in Fujian Province, composed the *Chu-fan chi* (1225), which is comparable to the *Periplus* as a guide to Indian Ocean trade. The *Chu-fan chi* provides a comprehensive account of peoples and goods traded, as well as the role of the monsoons in governing the rhythm of trade.

The rise of the Yuan (Mongol) dynasty (1271–1368) strengthened Chinese Indian Ocean trading connections. Marco Polo gives the following rich description of Quanzhou, in Fujian Province, which he calls "the splendid city of Zaiton, at which is the port for all the ships that arrive from India laden with costly wares and precious stones of great price and pearls of fine quality," in the late thirteenth century:

> It is also the port for the merchandise of Manzi, that is, of all the surrounding territory, so that the total amount of traffic in gems and other merchandise entering and leaving this port is a marvel to behold. From this city and its port goods are exported to the whole province of Manzi. And I assure you that for one spice ship that goes to Alexandria or elsewhere to pick up pepper for export to Christendom, Zaiton is visited by a hundred. For you must know that it is one of the two ports in the world with the biggest flow of merchandise.[26]

Polo's impression is verified by Ibn Battuta more than a half-century later, although there are many scholars who doubt whether the intrepid North African traveler actually visited the Chinese port. Nevertheless, he writes that "the port of Zaytún is one of the largest in the world, or perhaps the very largest. I saw in it about a hundred large junks; as for small junks, they could not be counted for the multitude."[27]

So when the Ming dynasty came to power in China in 1368, it is not surprising that they had imperial maritime ambitions. Official expeditions were led by Admiral Zheng He, who commanded seven voyages between 1405 and 1433. According to contemporary Chinese accounts, the purpose of these expeditions was both diplomatic and commercial. The fleets included the largest junks ever seen on the Indian Ocean, many of which had as many as nine masts and crews of five hundred men. These were referred to as *bao chuan*, or treasure ships, and are reported to have dwarfed all other vessels and some carried up to one thousand crew and passengers. These were genuine fleets, not simply convoys of merchant ships traveling together for safety, with hundreds of ships in three size categories and thousands of men. They were unprecedented in the history of the Indian Ocean.

The first three voyages visited ports in Southeast Asia and India, including Melaka and Calicut. The fourth voyage was the most ambitious, involving some 30,000 men, and sailing to Arabia via Hormuz. Nineteen different "countries" sent ambassadors back to China with gifts for the Ming emperor to promote trade. One of the most remarkable gifts was a giraffe that had been a gift from the ruler of Malindi, on the Kenya coast, to the king of Bengal and was carried to China for the emperor in 1414. In China the giraffe was regarded as an auspicious mythical beast known as a *qilin*.

A poem written to accompany a painting of the giraffe when it was presented at court on September 20 reads as follows:

> In a corner of the western seas, in the stagnant waters of a great morass,
> Truly was produced a *qilin*, whose shape was as high as fifteen feet,
> With the body of a deer and the tail of an ox, and a fleshy, boneless horn,
> With luminous spots like a red cloud or purple mist.
> Its hoofs do not tread on [living] beings and in its wanderings it carefully selects its ground,
> It walks in stately fashion and in its every motion it observes a rhythm,
> Its harmonious voice sounds like a bell or a musical tube.
> Gentle is this animal, that in all antiquity has been seen but once,
> The manifestation of its divine spirit rises up to heaven's abode.[28]

In the voyages of 1417 and 1421 Ming voyages visited the East African cities of Mogadishu, Malindi, whose ruler offered another giraffe to China, Mombasa, and Zanzibar. Finally, embarking on what proved to be the last Ming voyage in 1431, Zheng He's fleet revisited the major ports of Southeast Asia, Persia, the Red Sea, and Africa, but after departing Calicut Zheng He died on the return voyage. When the fleet reached

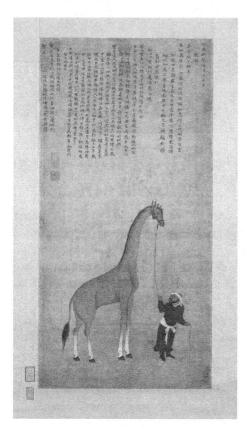

This giraffe, a present from the king of Malindi to the Chinese emperor in the fifteenth century, is led by a man in Arab-influenced clothing. Mistaken by the Chinese as a kind of mythical sacred animal called a qilin, *its appearance at court inspired this painting and accompanying poem.* National Palace Museum, Taiwan, Republic of China

China in 1433 it proved to be the last of its kind, as the Ming rulers turned increasingly inward and abandoned their outward-looking maritime diplomacy.

What did these extraordinary fleets represent? In the stone tablets that he had erected to commemorate his first six voyages, Zheng He declared that the treasure fleets had succeeded "in unifying seas and continents" and proclaimed that "the countries beyond the horizon from the ends of the earth have all become subjects . . . bearing precious objects and presents" to Ming China.[29] Somewhat different was the trilingual stone tablet placed at Galle, Sri Lanka, in 1411. Inscribed in Chinese, Tamil, and Persian, it called for peaceful trade and praised the Buddha, the Tamil God Tenevarai Nyanaar, and Allah. Nevertheless, the political reality was that imperial China sought and effected a tributary sovereignty over Sri Lanka for several decades. While the Chinese treasure fleets cannot be seen as the equivalent of the violent Portuguese intrusion into the Indian Ocean world at the end of the fifteenth century, less than seven decades after the voyage of the last Ming fleet, they were clearly motivated by political and economic ends. Moreover, the size of the fleets implied a level of force that no other Indian Ocean presence possessed.

It remains to say something about the persistence of piracy during the period during which the Indian Ocean was becoming a Muslim sea. Moving across the entire region from west to east, the first Muslim Arab occupation of the Dahlak Islands in 702 was precipitated by pirates who were based there. During the heyday of the Fatimid Caliphate its rulers kept a fleet of several ships to protect merchant ships as they traveled to the major Fatimid ports of Aydhab and Suakin on the western side of the Red Sea from local pirates, especially those based around the Dahlak Islands. According to Arab geographers, the island of Socotra had been known to be "a pirates' nest" as early as the tenth century, while the Central Asian traveler Ibn al-Mujāwir, who visited the island in the course of his travels in Arabia, wrote that "the life-style of the people of these coastal areas is [tied up] with pirates, since the latter come and stay with them for six months [at a time], selling them their loot."[30] Half a century later, Marco Polo confirms that at Socotra, "many corsairs put in at this island at the end of a cruise and pitch camp here and sell their booty."[31]

Along the Makran coast pirates known in Arabic sources as Bawarji were considered a menace to shipping in the Arabian Sea and the Gulf. In the tenth century, al-Masudi commented that the Bawarji threatened the India trade, while in the same century Buzurg describes a three-day sea battle against a massed fleet of these pirates. Centered on the ports of Daybul and Dwarka on the Kathiawar Peninsula of Gujarat, these pirates remained a thorn in the side of shipping right through the fifteenth century. Descriptions of these maritime raiders all come from writers located at the center of powerful regional Muslim states; whether those who carried out such acts regarded themselves as pirates remains an unanswered question.

One way to answer this question is to look at the question of piracy along the Malabar coast, an area identified by both Polo and Ibn Battuta as a favorite pirate haunt. On one occasion along this coast Ibn Battuta was traveling in an unprotected vessel that was attacked by pirates. No wonder, then, that he was convinced that the best guarantee of safety on the Indian Ocean was an armed escort, specifically a kind of broad galley that had "sixty oars and is covered with a roof during battle in order to protect the rowers from arrows and stones." He visited this vessel and writes that it also "had a complement of fifty rowers and fifty Abyssinian men-at-arms. These latter are the guarantors of safety on the Indian Ocean; let there be but one of them on a ship and it will be avoided by the Indian pirates and idolaters."[32] According to the great pilot Ibn Majid, the actual pirates along this coast "are a people ruled by their own rulers and number about a [sic] 1000 men and are a people of both land and sea with small boats (canoes)."[33] Other sources suggest that these maritime raiders belonged to a Hindu caste of sea fishermen who conducted their piracy on a seasonal basis as an established aspect of their economy. Thus, within their own communities these men were an integral part of society. In view of the domination of Malabar trade by merchants associated with politically powerful ports of trade, their commitment to inserting themselves into this lucrative commerce by force—that is, by piracy—comes as no surprise.

When he described the South China Sea trade route in about 800, geographer Chia Tan reported an area that lay "three days sailing westwards out of the Straits [of Melaka] to Ko-Ko-seng-ti Kuo, many of whose people were devoted to robbery and plunder, and were much feared by those who travel in ships."[34] Not surprisingly, royal protection of the sea lanes was an important policy and practice for the rulers of Srivijaya and those of east Java in the eleventh and twelfth centuries. Nevertheless, when Ibn Battuta reached maritime Southeast Asia in the middle of the fourteenth century he reports of the port of Qáqula, which is possibly located on the western coast of the Malayan Peninsula, that "we found there a number of junks ready for making piratical raids, and also for dealing with any junks that might attempt to resist their exactions, for they impose a tribute on each junk [calling at that place]."[35] A fourteenth-century Chinese source provides the following vivid description of the threat of endemic piracy near Singapore, at the other end of the Melaka Strait, where "the inhabitants are addicted to piracy . . . when junks sail to the Western [Indian] Ocean the local barbarians allow them to pass unmolested but when on their return the junks reach *Chi-li-men* the sailors prepare their armour and padded screens as a protection against arrows for, of a certainty, some two or three hundred pirate praus will put out to attack them for several days."[36] Indeed, by the fifteenth century Palembang, formerly the main port for Srivijaya, had become a major center for piracy.

On the return leg of his first voyage in 1407 Zheng He confronted the major pirate fleet of Chen Zuyi based at Palembang. According to contemporary Chinese sources, although Chen Zuyi sent tribute to the Chinese emperor, he continued his disruptive acts of piracy. The full description of this engagement is recorded in the *Taizong Shilu* in these terms:

Grand Director Zheng He, who had gone as envoy to the countries of the Western Ocean, returned holding in fetters the pirate Chen Zuyi and others. Originally Zheng He had arrived at the Old Harbor [of Palembang] and had encountered Chen Zuyi and the others, to whom he sent a messenger summoning them to submit. Chen Zuyi came down and pretended to submit, but kept his plans secret and actually intended to escape from the imperial fleet. Zheng He and his associates realized this and deployed their forces, preparing to stop him. Chen Zuyi, leading his forces, came out to plunder, and Zheng He sent forth his troops and did battle with him. Chen Zuyi was heavily defeated. Over five thousand of the pirate gang were killed, ten pirate ships were destroyed by burning and seven ships were captured, along with two forged seals made of copper. Chen Zuyi and two others were taken prisoner and delivered to the imperial capital, where all were ordered to be beheaded.[37]

Not only does this vivid account make clear the imperial motivations of the Ming treasure fleets, but it also bears witness to the military force assembled as part of state-directed Chinese maritime enterprise at this time. It equally stands as further evidence to the perils of Indian Ocean trade and the dynamic relationship between security and violence on both high seas and in ports. In a word, between piracy and shipwrecks, Indian Ocean maritime trade could be hazardous. Ibn al-Mujāwir wrote poignantly in the thirteenth century about the sense of great relief that an Indian Ocean merchant must have felt upon entering the secure port of Aden. "A man's return from the sea is like his rise from the grave, and the port is like the place of congregation on the Day of Judgment: there is questioning, and settlement of accounts, and weighing, and counting."[38] For many, the sense of calm captured by Ibn al-Mujāwir was about to be shattered by the arrival of the Portuguese in the Indian Ocean world.

CHAPTER 4

Intrusions and Transitions
in the Early Modern Period

On May 20, 1498, Vasco da Gama reached Calicut after a smooth passage from the East African coastal town of Malindi, where he had been advised about how to follow the monsoon by a Gujarati pilot. According to some sources, his first encounter in India was with two North African merchants from Tunis who reportedly spoke both Spanish and Italian. "The first greeting that he received was in these words: 'May the Devil take thee! What brought you hither?' They asked what he sought so far away from home, and he told them that we came in search of Christians and spices."[1]

True or not, Portuguese fleets had been seeking to outflank the control exercised over the spice trade by Venice and their Muslim counterparts who dominated the eastern Mediterranean for almost a century. Beginning with the conquest of the North African stronghold of Ceuta in 1415, Portuguese vessels had steadily made their way around the coast of western Africa until, in 1487–88, Bartolomeu Dias rounded the Cape of Good Hope. Emissaries to the Holy Land and Rome in the late medieval period from Christian Abyssinia, whose king was considered to be the mythical Prester John, had caused Western Christendom to hope to join forces with a Christian ally, now surrounded by Islam. So when Gama's small fleet of three ships anchored outside Calicut his allegedly declared goals are not surprising.

When they entered the Indian Ocean world, the Portuguese carried with them a deep antipathy to Islam and Muslims born of a crusading mentality. Yet Muslims were a familiar enemy. Hindus were unknown, which explains how it was that Gama thought "the city of Calicut is inhabited by Christians" and that "the king," meaning the Samudri-Raja/Zamorin, "was a Christian like himself."[2] Mistaking Hindu temples for Christian churches, Gama clearly misread the cultural differences the Portuguese encountered at Calicut. Eventually the Portuguese came

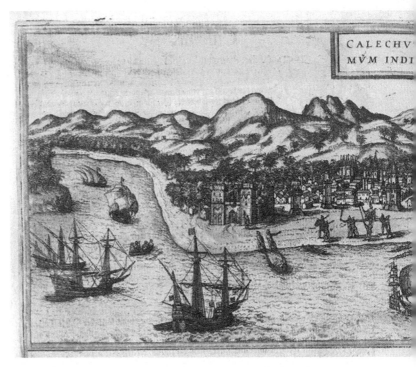

A 1572 image of Calicut reveals an extensive coastal settlement; most of the ships are Portuguese, but there is a regional vessel with lateen sails at the left in the river and also a man poling a dugout canoe. The elephant with a mahout standing on its back was probably used to haul timbers for the repair of ships, like those hauled up on shore.
National Library of Israel, Shapell Family Digitization Project and Hebrew University of Jerusalem, Department of Geography, Historic Cities Research Project

to distinguish between "Arabs," "Moors," meaning non-Arab Muslims, "Gentiles," meaning Hindus and Buddhists, and "Kaffirs," a term ironically adapted from the Arabic word for nonbelievers, to designate non-Muslim Africans. The basic prejudices they exhibited, however, marked attitudes that they shared with the European powers that followed them into the Indian Ocean world.

Gama's first experience at Calicut failed not because of racial prejudice, but because the Portuguese did not understand that the Samudri-Raja ruled over one of the most sophisticated commercial centers of the Indian Ocean. On May 29 Gama assembled a present for the king that consisted of "twelve pieces of lambel, four scarlet hoods, six hats, four strings of coral, a case containing six wash-hand basins, a case of sugar,

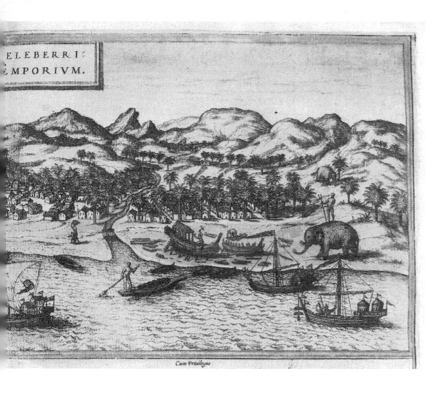

ELEBERRI:
MPORIVM.

Cum Privilegio

two casks of oil, and two of honey," essentially an assortment of minor trade goods. When the Samudri-Raja's trading representatives "saw the present they laughed at it, saying that it was not a thing to offer to a king, that the poorest merchant from Mecca, or any other part of India, gave more, and that if he wanted to make a present it should be in gold, as the king would not accept such things."[3] After Gama's misstep matters went from bad to worse, and the Portuguese left Calicut with a modest cargo of trade goods, although these brought the Portuguese Crown a great profit in Lisbon.

Although the Portuguese had forged an alliance with the king of Malindi, elsewhere on the Swahili coast the impetuous Gama had resorted to violence whenever he encountered reluctance to comply with his wishes. His experiences and the way in which he reported them resulted in the Portuguese embracing a bellicose approach to their attempt to seize control of the maritime trade of the Indian Ocean. When the much larger fleet of Pedro Álvares Cabral bombarded Calicut for two days in 1500 because the Samudri-Raja refused to expel all Muslims, it signaled the beginning of a long period of transition in Indian Ocean history. Nevertheless, as a single event Cabral's action was scarcely different from Zheng

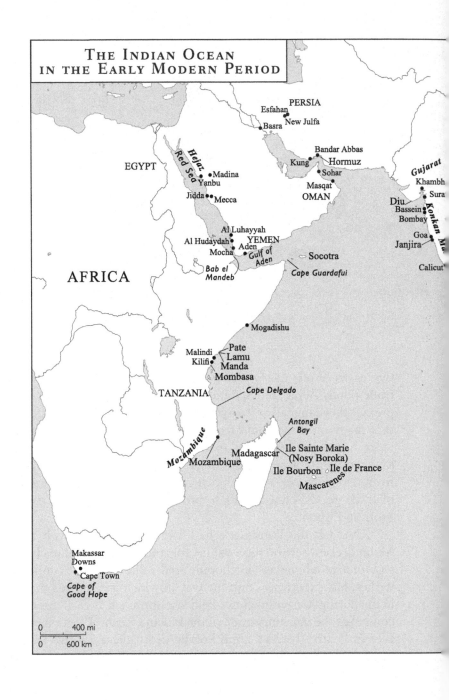

THE INDIAN OCEAN
IN THE EARLY MODERN PERIOD

PERSIA

Esfahan
New Julfa
Basra

EGYPT

Hejaz
Red Sea

Madina
Yanbu
Jidda Mecca

Bandar Abbas
Kung   Hormuz
Sohar
Masqat
OMAN

Gujarat

Khambh
Sura

Diu
Bassein
Bombay

Goa
Janjira

Konkan Ma

Al Luhayyah
Al Hudaydah   YEMEN
Mocha   Aden
Gulf of
Aden

Socotra

Calicut

Bab el
Mandeb

Cape Guardafui

AFRICA

Mogadishu

Malindi   Pate
Kilifi   Lamu
Manda
Mombasa

TANZANIA   Cape Delgado

Antongil
Bay

Mozambique

Mozambique

Madagascar

Ile Sainte Marie
(Nosy Boroka)
Ile Bourbon   Ile de France

Mascarenes

Makassar
Downs
Cape Town
Cape of
Good Hope

0   400 mi

0   600 km

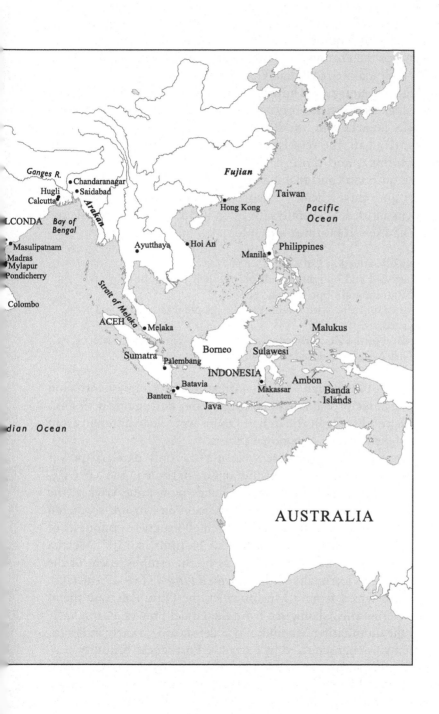

Ganges R.

Chandaranagar
Hugli • Saidabad
Calcutta

Arakan

LCONDA   Bay of
          Bengal

Masulipatnam

Madras
Mylapur
Pondicherry

Colombo

Strait of Melaka

ACEH   • Melaka

Sumatra   Palembang

Banten

Java

Batavia

INDONESIA

Borneo

Sulawesi

Makassar

Ambon

Malukus

Banda
Islands

Fujian

Hong Kong

Taiwan

Pacific
Ocean

Ayutthaya   • Hoi An

Manila •   Philippines

dian Ocean

AUSTRALIA

He's attack on Palembang less than a century previously. Unlike the Chinese, however, who seemed content after Palembang to exercise their influence nonviolently, equipped with the ability to fire cannon from on board their ships the Portuguese continued to employ violence in seeking to establish their mastery of Indian Ocean commerce.

Two Arab accounts reveal how the Portuguese actions were regarded by the Muslims. A sixteenth-century Hadrami chronicle refers to seaborne attacks launched by the Portuguese in 1502–3 in these terms: "In this year (Radjab) the vessels of the Frank appeared at sea en route for India, Hormuz, and those parts. They took about seven vessels, killing those on board and making some prisoner. This was their first action, may god curse them."[4] According to Ibn Majid's last major work, a poem entitled "al-Sofaliya" written in 1535, by which time the Portuguese had seized Hormuz and Jidda,

> [The Franks] arrived at Calicut . . .
> There they sold and bought, and displayed their power, bought off
>   the Zamorin, and oppressed the people.
> Hatred of Islam came with them! And the people were afraid and
>   anguished.
> And the land of the Zamorin was snatched away from that of Mecca,
>   and Guardafui was closed to travelers.[5]

In a very real sense, although Muslim antipathy to Portuguese intrusion was expressed in reciprocal religio-cultural terms, Portuguese actions in disturbing peaceful trade in the Indian Ocean were little different from the actions of generations of regional pirates.

As it happens, the Portuguese were not the only external power seeking to exercise dominance over Indian Ocean trade in the early sixteenth century. Within two decades of Gama's pioneering voyage, the Ottoman Empire sought to stake out a position as Muslim sovereign over the Islamic Indian Ocean. Prodded by the Portuguese conquests of strategic Indian Ocean choke points such as Hormuz in 1507, Melaka in 1511, and Columbo in 1518, as well as by the establishment of the grandiosely named Viceroyalty of the *Estado da Índia* at Goa, which the Portuguese also seized from a Muslim ruler, the Ottomans saw themselves as delivering this Islamic sea from the infidel Franks. Particularly galling was the humiliating Mamluk naval defeat at Diu early in February 1509 that was characterized by excessive Portuguese brutality.

Following their conquest of Mamluk Egypt in 1517, the Ottomans developed a comprehensive strategy to gather intelligence and develop their navy so as to be able to recapture control of the Indian Ocean seaways for

Islam and, more to the point, for the Ottoman Empire. Over the course of the sixteenth century these two great powers—one land-based but aspiring to maritime superiority, the other a small European kingdom with a maritime empire that spanned two oceans—struggled to defeat each other and gain command over the wealth of the Indian Ocean trade.

The Luso-Ottoman rivalry extended from the Red Sea as far east as northern Sumatra. Although the Portuguese failed in their attempts to take Aden, and in 1511 abandoned a foothold on Socotra after only five years, they continued to threaten Muslim control of the Red Sea for the first half of the sixteenth century by regularly dispatching naval patrols to the Gulf of Aden and deep into the Red Sea itself. To meet this challenge the Ottomans seized control of Suakin in 1524, Mocha in 1535, Aden, first in 1538 and finally in 1549, as well as fortifying the critical Hejaz port of Jidda in 1525. This short period of struggle to control the Red Sea undoubtedly affected negatively the flow of commerce through this critical arm of the Indian Ocean, but by about 1540 trade appears to have regained its normal rhythm.

According to a report by Portuguese chronicler Diogo de Couto, a Portuguese patrol waiting outside the Bab el Mandeb in 1562 was decidedly unsuccessful, noting that "they saw more than sixty different [Muslim] vessels without ever being able to reach even one of them. This was because [the Portuguese vessels] were near the shore, and [the merchant ships] came in from the sea with the wind fully at their backs. It was therefore impossible either to catch them or to follow them inside [the mouth of the Red Sea], for [the Portuguese] dared not enter the straits for fear of risking the loss of their own ships."[6] Thus, although the Portuguese patrols amounted to a form of state piracy, this particular one was rendered ineffective as much by the monsoon as by the failure of its commander.

The Ottomans generally did not seek to challenge the Portuguese in the open seas. Their fleet consisted primarily of galleys or galliots, which combined oars with sails, that were most effective near the coast and where their pace and maneuverability could overcome the size and firepower of the Portuguese sailing vessels. In addition to the Red Sea standoff, once the Ottomans took control of Basra in 1546 a diplomatic *modus vivendi* evolved with the Portuguese at Hormuz. Nevertheless, direct conflicts did occur as both the Ottomans and the Portuguese sought to draw upon local allies to give them an advantage in the longer-term competition for control of the Indian Ocean.

In 1538 the Ottomans sent a massive fleet of seventy vessels into the Indian Ocean to challenge the Portuguese in western India and Southeast

Asia. It did not succeed. The Mappila corsairs who were supposed to challenge the Portuguese along the Malabar and Konkan coast were defeated before the Ottoman fleet set sail, while an attack on Melaka by Muslim allies in northern Sumatra likewise failed. The main battle was played out before Diu, which the Portuguese had wrested from the Sultan of Gujarat during the latter's short-lived repulse of the expanding Mughal Empire only three years previously. The Ottoman fleet laid siege to the island-fortress of Diu for six weeks and almost brought the Portuguese to their knees, but failures of leadership and of coordination with local allies caused the Ottomans to withdraw without success.

In the early 1550s the Ottomans again mounted a major offensive against the Portuguese, this time focusing their efforts on the massive fortress at Hormuz, at the entrance to the Gulf. Once again the expedition met with disastrous failure. The Ottoman fleet withdrew to Basra before attempting to return to its home port at Suez. In the largest open sea battle between these imperial rivals, the Ottoman galleys commanded by Murad Beg almost destroyed the Portuguese fleet. Aided by a sudden drop in the wind that left the Portuguese sailing vessels helpless, the Ottomans devastated the Portuguese until a just-as-sudden resumption of the wind enabled the Portuguese to regroup and counterattack their Ottoman enemies, who withdrew again to Basra. Under a new commander, Seydi Ali Reis, in 1554 the Ottoman fleet set out once more to return to Suez. Thinking they had slipped the Portuguese fleet at Hormuz, the Ottomans rowed across the Hormuz Strait to Masqat where the faster Portuguese sailing vessels had preceded them and organized a murderous ambush. The Portuguese destroyed six Ottoman galleys in the battle and two of the remaining nine were wrecked in their escape into the stormy open sea. In his memoir Seydi Ali wrote, "As compared to these awful tempests, the foul weather in the Western seas is mere child's play, and their towering billows are as drops of water compared to those of the Indian sea."[7] The Ottoman commander finally led the remnant of his fleet into a friendly port on the western Indian coast, where they were abandoned and scrapped, while he made his way overland to Istanbul. Nothing was left of the Ottoman fleet.

The crushing defeat did not end this great rivalry. Based on their control of the Islamic Holy Lands, the Ottomans fashioned themselves as protectors of the faith in the Indian Ocean world. Like the Portuguese, they also desired to control the rich spice trade of the Malukus. Accordingly, the Ottomans sought to challenge the Portuguese position in Southeast Asia, in particular their control of Melaka. They did this by wooing the Muslim Sultanate of Aceh in northern Sumatra, which plied

This Portuguese rendering of the great sea battle in the harbor of Masqat in 1554 depicts both the Portuguese caravels, with the names of their commanders by each ship, and the smaller, oared Ottoman galleys. The setting of Masqat, surrounded by high mountains, is an accurate, if stylized, representation. The Pierpont Morgan Library, New York. MS M.525, fols. 16v-17

a handsome direct annual trade with the Ottoman-controlled Red Sea and Gujarat. Aceh had already failed once to seize Melaka, but by mid-century much of its trade involved the importation of armaments. Although it was nominally a vassal to the Portuguese, Aceh sent an emissary to Istanbul in 1562 and two years later an Ottoman representative named Lutfi reached Aceh, where he apparently became a focus for pan-Islamic and anti-Portuguese sentiment. Lutfi returned to Istanbul in 1566 carrying a letter from the Sultan of Aceh that Lutfi probably drafted and that declared Aceh to be "one of Your Majesty's own villages, and I too am one of your servants."[8]

At the same time diplomatic exchanges between the Ottoman Empire and Portugal appeared to be heating up, as Sultan Suleiman the Magnificent wrote to King Sebastião:

> It has been reported that the Muslim pilgrims and merchants coming from India by sea have been molested and abused in direct violation of the desired peace agreement between us. . . . If it is truly your desire to bring peace and security to those lands, then as soon as this Imperial

Ferman arrives you must cease all of your attacks at sea against merchants and pilgrims. . . . If you are still set on pursuing the path of rebellion, then with the help of God Almighty we will do everything necessary to restore order to those lands.[9]

Although nothing came of either the Ottoman or the Acehnese threat to Portugal's Estado da India at this time, the language of Suleiman's letter to the Portuguese monarch serves as a reminder, yet again, that the Portuguese were essentially cast as piratical interlopers in the largely Muslim Indian Ocean world of the sixteenth century.

The final episode in this historical drama played itself out not in Southeast Asia nor in Gujarat, where the Mughal conquest of the independent sultanate in 1573, including Surat, which had particularly close connections to Ottoman merchants, created a different set of challenges for the Ottoman Empire. Instead, the denouement occurred where the Portuguese intrusion into the Indian Ocean had begun, on the Swahili coast. The key Ottoman figure was a dashing sea captain named Mir Ali Beg, who was based at Mocha on the southwest coast of Yemen. In 1581 he made a daring raid on Masqat with only three ships, sacking the city and capturing three vessels and a large amount of booty. According to a seventeenth-century Portuguese chronicler, "in the opening and closing of an eye he entered the town a pauper and came out again a rich man."[10]

Over the next few years rising Muslim agitation against the Portuguese, including another Ottoman-assisted attack on Melaka, prompted new Ottoman imperial ambitions of liberating the Islamic Indian Ocean lands from the Christian infidels and against their Mughal Muslim rivals. The ambitious governor of Yemen sought to take advantage of the rising Islamic tide by liberating the East African coast, which had close trade relations with the Ottoman Red Sea, from its nominal Portuguese suzerainty. He ordered Mir Ali Beg to reconnoiter East African waters.

Although the Ottoman commander arrived in January 1586 with only a single galliot and some eighty men, his mission met with enthusiastic reception at towns from Mogadishu to Pate, each of which promised men, money, and local shipping to support Ottoman intervention. Because the Portuguese commander at Malindi decided not to challenge him, Mir Ali Beg managed to seize several Portuguese vessels, eventually amassing a fleet of two dozen vessels from almost nothing. He received fealty from every Swahili town except Malindi and returned to Mocha on the Southwest Monsoon with a large amount of booty, including gold, ambassadors from Mombasa, Kilifi, and Pate, and sixty Portuguese captives. The king of Malindi, whose town had hitched its star to the

Portuguese from their first appearance in the Indian Ocean, warned the Portuguese at Goa that if Mir Ali Beg returned with a larger fleet, as he had promised to do, and the king of Mombasa fulfilled his promise to build a fort at Mombasa, the entire coast could be lost to the Ottomans. Were this to happen, the annual passage of the *carreira da India*—the royal fleet linking Portuguese Asia to Lisbon—would be seriously jeopardized.

In December 1588 Mir Ali Beg's second and larger fleet embarked from Mocha for the Swahili coast, where his reception was as enthusiastic as three years before. Alerted to his expedition by its spies in Yemen, the Portuguese organized a large fleet that included three times as many soldiers as Mir Ali Beg commanded to sail from Goa to East Africa. The battle was joined in March 1589 at the island-city state of Mombasa, Malindi's chief rival on the coast. The smaller Ottoman force was caught between the powerful Portuguese fleet and a fearsome African mainland army of so-called Zimba who temporarily allied themselves with the Portuguese. Together they devastated the Ottomans and their Mombasa allies. The Portuguese sacked Manda for supporting the Ottomans and publicly executed the king of Lamu and several leading citizens of Pate and Kilifi. The faithful ruler of Malindi received Mombasa as a reward for his support. Mir Ali Beg and some of his men were captured, the latter serving the rest of their days as slaves in Portuguese India. Mir Ali Beg was sent from Goa to Lisbon and converted to Christianity. The withdrawal of the Ottoman governor of Basra in 1596, followed by the loss of Mocha in 1636 and Aden in 1645, marked the complete end to Ottoman pretensions to Indian Ocean empire.

Unwilling to chance defending further challenges to their precarious hold on the Swahili coast without a solid base, the Portuguese determined to build a fortress stronghold at their new headquarters at Mombasa that was equal to the monumental Fort São Sebastião at Mozambique Island, which they began in 1558 and finally completed in 1583. They wasted no time and initiated the building of Fort Jesus in 1593, rapidly completing construction in 1596. Cape Delgado became the boundary between the Portuguese Captaincies of Mombasa and Mozambique, both of which still were subordinate to a Portuguese Viceroy at Goa. It remains today the coastal boundary between modern mainland Tanzania and Mozambique.

As newcomers to the trading systems of the Indian Ocean, the Portuguese soon realized that they could not compete directly with well-established indigenous merchant networks. Instead, operating from fortified points around the Indian Ocean littoral, they sought to rake off profits by imposing port taxes, requiring Crown licenses or passports known as *cartazes* on non-Portuguese merchant vessels, and forcibly inhibiting dangerous rivals that they defined either as "infidels" or "pirates." In addition, unofficial Portuguese settlers married locally and became go-betweens with indigenous traders, as well as coastal traders themselves, not unlike their Arab and Indian predecessors in the Indian Ocean world. In Portuguese centers of power like Mozambique Island, Diu, and Melaka, where they had aggressively attacked Gujarati and Arab Muslim traders and pushed them out of the local market, different Hindu associations of traders took advantage of the situation that weakened their Muslim rivals to work with the Portuguese. Gujarati *baniyas*, Hindu and Jain members of this trading caste, from Diu became dominant traders at Mozambique, while Tamil Keling merchants from the Coromandel coast, as well as non-Muslim Chinese, became increasingly influential communities in Melaka during the sixteenth century. Elsewhere, however, Indian Ocean trading continued much as it had before the Portuguese intrusion.

In the course of a century the Portuguese had without question effected change in the Indian Ocean world. They had introduced a novel form of state violence to seaborne trade, new ship designs that some Indian Ocean boat builders sought to adapt to their own needs, and a form of Portuguese Creole that had evolved first in the Atlantic world and became a lingua franca for many Indian Ocean traders and in many Indian Ocean communities, even beyond formal Portuguese rule. But despite linking the Indian Ocean directly to the Atlantic, the Portuguese had not substantially altered historical patterns of trade or the lives of its indigenous inhabitants. Christianity had few converts outside of Portuguese Goa, and the Holy Roman Church had failed miserably in trying to impose its form of Christianity on Orthodox Ethiopia in the sixteenth century. At the end of that century, then, the Portuguese Crown seemed secure in its ability to control the open seas of the Indian Ocean from its fortified coastal bastions. Most of these were on islands or peninsulas, with very little in the way of continental domination, except for mainland conquests to the immediate north and south of Goa. Portugal's was in every sense a seaborne empire or thalassocracy. It was also about to be challenged by a series of European rivals.

The familiar story of seventeenth-century European rivalries in the Indian Ocean focuses on the roles played by their different trading companies and their private employees, followed by the transition to genuine colonial domination from about the middle of the eighteenth century. Many different European private merchants, corsairs, and freebooters sought to break into the Indian Ocean commercial arena opened up by the Portuguese, especially after the Spanish incorporation of the Portuguese Crown made Portugal the enemy of both England and the Netherlands. But the main challenges came when these nations organized their merchants into chartered companies to rival the royal monopoly that dominated the Portuguese venture. First off the mark in 1600 was the English joint-stock East India Company (EIC). It was followed two years later by the Dutch East India Company, the *Verenigde Oostindische Compagnie* (VOC). Drawing upon the burgeoning capitalist economy of the Netherlands, the VOC was organized to trade and earn profit. It was also much more aggressive than the EIC and took the initiative in challenging the Portuguese in the Indian Ocean.

The Dutch and English shared many of the same prejudices of their Portuguese rivals regarding Muslims and other non-Christian peoples of the Indian Ocean world. In the words of a metropolitan VOC administrator writing in 1669, "We have had ample occasion to learn that people in the East Indies are in general of an evil and treacherous nature. They do not have the slightest scruple to break any commitment and are imbued with a deep hatred for Christians."[11] In the end, however, the main concern of both companies was to drive trade. The Dutch conquered Melaka in 1641, Colombo in 1658, and all the Malabar ports in the 1660s. In addition, they took command of a small Javanese port named Jakarta in 1619 and renamed it Batavia, which became the center of VOC activities in the Indian Ocean. Dutch success was built on their engagement with the so-called country trade or inter-Asian trade that drove the internal markets of the Indian Ocean, drawing upon the shifting hinterlands where goods were produced and exchanging them overseas or overland for other goods. The direct trade to Europe was laid over this more deeply rooted trade. Finally, to secure their shipping from the Atlantic into the Indian Ocean in 1652 they also established a station and colony at Cape Town. Although Portugal had toyed with the establishment of a foothold on the African coast to the south of Sofala in the previous century, this decision by the Dutch marked the real integration of South Africa into the Indian Ocean world.

The goal of the VOC was to establish a monopoly of the spice trade—cloves, nutmeg, and mace—and while the Dutch definitely had success in this sector, their control was initially never absolute. When they failed to achieve their ends regarding nutmeg and mace in the Banda Islands, they decimated the indigenous population and in 1621 replaced them with slaves, loyal Dutch, and willing Indonesians. From the mid-seventeenth century they again employed raw violence to eradicate clove production from the Malukus, where indigenous merchants often evaded Dutch

As the Dutch sought to control the spice trade, the development of more detailed local maps, like this eighteenth-century one of the Malukus, was important to the Dutch imperial project. The image of a seated man, perhaps a local chief, with a spear in his hand and boxes of goods at his feet may suggest the nature of exchange in the Malukus. Map Collection, Rare Books and Special Collections, Northern Illinois University Libraries

control, and reestablish production on Ambon, which was under firm VOC control. Because its cultivation was widespread in both Malabar and Indonesia, the VOC was unable to control production of pepper. Instead, they labored to dominate the coastal markets for the pepper trade, which they were also able largely to achieve by the late seventeenth century.

In addition to monopolizing the spice trade, the VOC responded to the growing Euro-American appetite for coffee. Originally cultivated in highland Ethiopia and Yemen, the international market for coffee was first driven by Ottoman and Persian demand. In the seventeenth and eighteenth centuries, the Yemeni ports of Mocha, Al Hudaydah, and Al Luhayyah were the main outlets for coffee traders, the most well known being Mocha. In the mid-eighteenth century German traveler Carsten Niebuhr recorded the following legend about the city's origins, which focus on a venerable Sufi saint, Shaykh Ali b. Umar al-Qirshi al-Shadhili:

This nineteenth-century German drawing of the flower and fruit of the clove plant is emblematic of how European expansion inspired new generations of naturalists seeking to control knowledge of indigenous plants. From Köhler's *medizinal-Pflanzen in naturgetreuen Abbildungen mit kurz erläuterndem Texte: Atlas zur Pharmacopoea germanica, austriaca, belgica, danica, helvetica, hungarica, rossica, suecica, neerlandica, British pharmacopoeia, zum Codex medicamentarius, sowie zur Pharmacopoeia of the United States of America* by Hermann Köhler, courtesy of Biodiversity Heritage Library, http://www .biodiversitylibrary.org, and the Missouri Botanical Garden, Peter H. Raven Library

A ship bound from India to Jidda cast anchor, one day, about four hundred years since, in these latitudes. The crew, observing a hut in the desert, had the curiosity to go and see it. The Scheh [*shaykh*] gave those strangers a kind of reception, and regaled them with coffee, of which he was very fond himself, and to which he ascribed great virtues. The Indians who were unacquainted with the use of coffee, thought that this hot liquid might cure the master of their ship, who was ill. Schaedeli assured them, that, not only should he be cured by the efficacy of his prayers, and of the coffee, but that if they would land their cargo there, they might dispose of it to considerable advantage.[12]

As for the Dutch, in 1696 they introduced coffee plants to Indonesia and in 1725 initiated a system of forced cultivation with annual quotas in the highlands of West Java, eventually to be followed by areas under their control in Sumatra. Dutch success on the world market may be measured by the adoption of "java" as a popular name for coffee, just as "mocha" suggested a superior variety of this stimulating beverage.

Although slavery was an ancient institution everywhere and small-scale slave trading was endemic in the Indian Ocean world, after the failed ninth-century Iraqi experiment with slavery it was the Dutch who first employed slaves in agricultural slavery. A census taken in 1688 counted the total enslaved population of the Dutch Indian Ocean possessions of the Cape, Ceylon, and Indonesia at about 70,000 individuals, which was supplied by an annual slave trade of between 3,730 and 6,430. Captives were drawn from East Africa and Madagascar, from India, and from Southeast Asia. In the middle decades of the seventeenth century the largest numbers came from the Arakan/Bengal and Coromandel coastal regions of India. In addition to the Dutch slave trade between Coromandel and Indonesia, independent Aceh imported many slaves from Coromandel to work on rice production during this period. Although not all bonded laborers worked in agriculture, their employment there was a harbinger of things to come in the Indian Ocean colonial world.

As the Dutch worked steadily to monopolize the spice trade that had drawn them to this part of the world, for most of the seventeenth century the British remained a much less active participant in the main currents of Indian Ocean trade. Instead, they focused their attention on gaining a foothold on the Indian subcontinent, allying themselves with local mercantile and political partners to acquire a piece of the region's rich trade. They built a fort at Madras (now Chennai), in 1639, and acquired Bombay (now Mumbai), from Portugal in 1667; in 1690 they received a license to establish a parallel trading center on the Hugli River at Calcutta (now Kolkata). They also developed a chain of trading factories in other ports around peninsular India, including one at Surat in 1612. With a firm array of bases in coastal India, from about 1680 to 1740 the British became a much more important factor in Indian Ocean trade, exploiting the textile trade from India as well as developing new trade in tea and opium to Indonesia and, eventually, China.

The withdrawal of Ming China from the Indian Ocean after the death of Admiral Zheng He in the second quarter of the fifteenth century ensured that a potentially major Asian navy was not a factor in the early modern period. Nevertheless, except for the chaotic period that precipitated and followed the collapse of the Ming dynasty in 1744 and its replacement by the Manchu Qing dynasty, China remained an integral part of the easternmost branch of Indian Ocean commerce, despite an imperial ban on private trading from Fujian ports. In fact, from about 1570 to 1630, a period when the Ming reversed the ban on private Chinese trade to the south, the number of licensed Chinese junks increased significantly to more than one hundred at the end of the sixteenth century. Because Europeans were denied access to China until 1684, and even then their ships were subject to very high tariffs, the China trade continued to be dominated by Chinese and Chinese-crewed Southeast Asian junks. After the slump associated with the dynastic change in China, from about 1680 forward Chinese trade with Southeast Asia expanded significantly.

Because many overseas Chinese merchants had fought against the new Manchu rulers under the leadership of Ming loyalist Zheng Chenggong, who had seized Taiwan from the Dutch and made it his base in 1662, in the first half of the eighteenth century the Chinese state remained ambivalent about how to regulate its overseas trade. For example, it attempted to control overseas Chinese traders by a 1727 regulation that required Chinese traders to return to China after three years abroad, which many merchants avoided. Recognizing that trade to insular Southeast Asia was important to China, the Manchu governor of Fujian Province recommended in the early 1750s that transgressors should be allowed to return home "provided that their real reason for not returning within the time allowed was their inability to close their accounts."[13]

Chinese merchants were ubiquitous throughout both mainland and insular Southeast Asia in the early modern period. From their coastal ports Chinese merchants penetrated hinterland supply lines that fed the overseas markets. By about 1630 the Dutch depended upon Chinese merchants to supply them with the goods they sought in exchange for cloth in Southeast Asia, while Chinese junks dominated about half of local shipping networks. Large Chinese merchant communities flourished at Ayutthaya in Siam, Banten in Java, and Hoi An in Vietnam. In Spanish Manila, their numbers had reached 23,000 before a terrible massacre in 1603, only the first of many against the Chinese in the Spanish Philippines, decimated their population. During the earlier decades of the seventeenth century Chinese merchants tended to marry local women and to integrate themselves with local society, but toward the end of the century, perhaps as a combined consequence of the official requirement that overseas merchants regularly return to China and the Dutch preference for separateness in Indonesia, this process soon declined. Still, many Chinese in the trading centers of indigenous Southeast Asian states continued to localize themselves, while those in Dutch urban areas like Batavia retained their "foreign" character.

In both settings it is remarkable that Chinese merchants became tax farmers for state revenue collection. By securing a reliable annual source of revenue for the state, whatever its provenance, Chinese business became ever more closely associated with the political elites of both regional and colonial administrations. Nevertheless, resentment against Chinese economic domination in Batavia, where they were almost 40 percent of the population at the end of the seventeenth century, resulted in a pogrom against them in 1740. In the aftermath the Dutch relocated the remaining Chinese to a Chinatown outside the main city walls.

An ironic consequence of European competition in the Indian Ocean during the early modern period is that every player regarded itself as the rightful claimant to domination and its rivals as pirates. To take only one example, according to the Portuguese viceroy, writing in January 1698, "The sea is full of pirates, which will result in the ruin of commerce and—if robbery continues like this—its total destruction and it is rumored with good grounds that all pirates are Englishmen and they go to Bombay to sell the treasures they have robbed. And if our frigates try to seize them they show us letter-patents of the East India Company, so that we cannot do them any harm."[14] Apparently, for the viceroy a Portuguese cartaz signaled a legitimate merchant ship, while its British equivalent amounted to a legal dodge to enable piracy. By contrast, to indigenous merchants and sailors it was the Portuguese who were the pirates.

By the 1680s eastern Madagascar, which lay beyond the reach of any European claimant to Indian Ocean sea power, had become the principal world base for a collection of pirates who had been driven out of the Caribbean. Although most captains were British, their crews included French, Dutch, and Danish sailors. Most were pirates by trade; others were honest seamen who had been pressed into piracy after their ships had been captured. Secure in their coastal strongholds, these maritime raiders sallied out to attack shipping across the northwestern Indian Ocean and into the Red Sea. They indiscriminately preyed upon both Muslim and European shipping, depending on the circumstances, the potential spoils, and the particular connections of individual pirate captains. For them piracy was their business; their notoriety was widespread.

To take only one example, the rich coffee trade of Mocha attracted shipping from all over the Indian Ocean and piracy in the Red Sea was both rife and multinational. In 1661–62 a Dutch vessel seized an Indian merchantman bound for Mocha, only releasing it after payment of a steep ransom. According to "An Account of the Attack by the Band of Hollanders and English of the Christian Nations, on the Port of Mocha," written by the governor of that port, al-Hasan b. al-Mutahharal al-Djarmuzi, when the Yemeni authorities tried to negotiate, the Dutch seized their envoys. "Turning to such Muslim shipping as was found off the coast, they sank and burned it, looting all they were able." Then, when the Muslims attempted to counterattack, the Dutch interlopers overwhelmed their ship and took or burned their goods. "As for the large vessel," al-Djarmuzi writes, "a galliot, and two vessels belonging to the Indians, these they burned along with four sambooks; then they put back to sea."[15]

European piracy in the Red Sea had serious implications for any European traveler. In August 1700 an English traveler named William Daniel, who was carrying official letters for the EIC from London to Surat, found himself at Yanbu, the Arabian port for Medina. When he was brought before the local Ottoman governor, he records, "he was inform'd I was a pyrat and a spy, going to joyn and give information to those of Madagascar, who had lately taken a ship near Mocha in which he and his relations were concern'd, and now he thought he could not do himself greater justice than to have satisfaction of me."[16]

Like the pirates of the Caribbean, the exploits of the Madagascar pirates in the late seventeenth century make for exciting popular history and fiction. What is most interesting from the perspective of the Indian Ocean world, however, is the social transformation that accompanied the settlement of European pirates along the coast of eastern Madagascar. In a process that recalls the integration of Arabs and Persians into what became Swahili and Mappila societies, or smaller scattered communities in the eastern Indian Ocean, individual pirates gradually settled in local coastal villages from Tamatave (today Toamasina) south to Antongil Bay, where the small Ile Sainte Marie (today Nosy Boraha) became the center for the stockpiling and marketing of goods seized by pirates of this community. Most pirate settlers married local women and established commercial and political relations with the different local polities. In several cases the immigrant men became local rulers by exploiting the distribution of the wealth they had accumulated and by making astute marriages. The children of these unions between pirates and Malagasy women became known as Malata, mulattos, or Zana-Malata, children of mulattos. Not surprisingly, there was initially no political unity along the pirate coast, while their cumulative wealth increased on profits from trading slaves to the Mascarene Islands, which under French rule had begun to develop plantation economies with a resulting demand for labor from the second quarter of the eighteenth century.

Despite their diverse origins, in the 1710s the Zana-Malata provided a generation of political leadership that precipitated the emergence of what is today the second largest Malagasy ethnic group, the Betsimisaraka. The process began with the political struggle for control of the coast between a coalition of indigenous northerners or Antavaratra and a parallel grouping of southerners or Antatsimo. In this contest the Zana-Malata joined forces with the Antavaratra. In about 1712, a Zana-Malata leader named Ratsimilaho, the son of an English pirate named Tom and a Malagasy royal daughter, emerged as leader of the northern alliance and led them to a defeat of the southerners. The victorious alliance then assumed the name of Betsimisaraka or "the many inseparable" and Ratsimilaho was elected their king with the throne name of Ramaromanampo, "he who rules over many." European traders knew him as Tom Similaho, a name that acknowledges his dual parentage. The Betsimisaraka kingdom was more a confederacy than a unified state, and it was weakened by competition along the coast for control of the slave trade to the Mascarenes. Political unity was ephemeral and the kingdom fell apart after the death of Ramaromanampo in 1750. Yet by then the ethnic identity associated with the name of Betsimisaraka had become well established and the group retained a reputation as fierce warriors, no doubt a heritage of their pirate ancestors.

Notwithstanding the imperial competition as well as the great violence that characterized the methods of each of these intruders, the essential patterns of Indian Ocean commerce remained in the hands of indigenous networks. Foremost among these were Gujaratis, whose capital and shipping dominated the trade in spices from Southeast Asia, textiles and indigo from northwestern India, as well as the return carriage of bullion and specie from the Red Sea. The draining of precious metals from the Atlantic economies, which were now exploiting the silver mines of South America, to the East as payment for spices and the textiles of China and India was a persistent feature of international trade in the early modern period. Gujarati shipping also commanded the annual traffic generated by the *hajj*, the annual pilgrimage by Muslims to the Holy Lands of the Hejaz. With Khambhat as their principal port until the Mughal conquest of Gujarat determined Surat as the official Mughal maritime outlet for Gujarat, the network of Gujarati baniyas stretched from Mocha in Yemen to Aceh in Sumatra.

As members of a group of Hindu and Jain merchant families, baniyas provided nearly all of the financing of the Gujarati commercial networks. Like other communally defined trading groups, such as the Jewish traders who participated in the India trade in the thirteenth century, baniyas depended on a network of family and cultural intimates—whether locational, religious, or linguistic—to further their commercial interests. Credit was another institution on which Indian Ocean commerce depended. Although banks did not exist, bills of exchange, or *hundis*, served the same function for baniyas and other indigenous Indian Ocean traders. To an outsider, theirs was a closed enterprise. Writing in 1611, a frustrated VOC employee commented, "The *banias* keep their accounts on long scrolls of paper in secret signs and they are so secretive about their content that they will never show them to anybody. So they will have two books: one to show to outsiders and one showing the actual trade."[17]

Of course, not all Gujarati merchants were baniyas. In the early sixteenth century the wealthiest merchant and governor at Surat was a certain Malik Gopi, also known as Gopinath, who as a Hindu Brahmin belonged to a higher caste than the baniyas. Two distinct Ismaili Shia Muslim groups, the Khojas and Bohras, were also deeply involved in commerce, as were a smaller group of Sunni Bohras, including Mulla Abdul Ghafur, a fabulously wealthy merchant-shipper at Surat in the early seventeenth century. Ghafur was unusual not only for his exceptional wealth, but because he combined being a merchant with being the largest shipowner at Surat. Indeed, whereas most merchants were Hindu and Jain baniyas, most shipowners were Muslims. Late in the following century still another indigenous group, the Parsis, became notable merchants at Surat and subsequently at Bombay, where they forged a profitable alliance with the British East India Company.

Following the Portuguese seizure of Melaka and the ouster of Muslims from that city, Gujarati Muslims shifted their activities to the rival Muslim Sultanate of Aceh. Despite Ottoman pretensions to leading the Indian Ocean Muslim community by wooing Aceh, it was Gujarati Muslims based there who made it possible to bypass the Portuguese control of the spice trade between Southeast Asia and the Red Sea. In addition, among the great proponents of orthodox Islam in Sumatra in the seventeenth century was Nuruddin ar-Raniri, a Gujarati Sufi from a Hadhrami family who wrote a seven-volume history of the world and guide to Islamic monarchy, the *Bustan al-Salatin*, or Garden of Kings, in Malay. Before arriving in Aceh, Nuruddin had studied in Mecca; eventually he returned to Gujarat. His story reveals parallel Gujarati commercial and religious networks that operated in the Indian Ocean world during this era.

Another example of how commercial and sacred geographies coincided comes from a less prominent and relatively short-lived contemporaneous network. Lying midway between the important ports of the Coromandel and the mouths of the Ganges River in eastern India, Masulipatnam became the outlet port for the Sultanate of Golconda in the last quarter of the sixteenth century and part of a network of Bay of Bengal ports that collaborated to avoid Portuguese attempts to control trade from Melaka. One of the major Golconda court factions was Persian and its members soon came to dominate maritime trade from Masulipatnam. In the first half of the seventeenth century Persians occupied all the official posts at Masulipatnam and were its principal shipowners. While most of its trade was in the Bay of Bengal, an annual ship was sent under the flag of the Golconda sultan to the Red Sea.

By the 1630s, the sultan's ship from Masulipatnam typically had Dutch pilots and gunners, as well as occasional men provided by the English and even the Danes. When in 1622 the Portuguese lost Hormuz to a combined Safavid Persian and English attack, it was replaced as the major Gulf port by Bandar Abbas, on the Persian mainland. This turn of events encouraged Masulipatnam's Persian merchants to establish a new trading link between these two ports with permission granted in 1632 to the Sultan of Golconda by the Shah of Persia. Although the initial voyages met with limited commercial success, the route was apparently still worth pursuing for Persian merchant Mir Kamal-al-din. What is especially interesting is that when he sought the sultan's approval for a return voyage in 1635, the English at Surat reported "that hee may visit the toombe of a certaine Prophet unto which he is much devoted," presumably the shrine of a prominent Sufi saint.[18] Here again is evidence for the overlap between a commercial and a sacred geography.

The Masulipatnam–Bandar Abbas link was most successful in the 1640s and 1650s under the dominant figure of Mir Muhammad Sayyid Ardestani, who originally came to Golconda as a horse trader from Esfahan, capital of Safavid Persia. He soon became a successful diamond merchant and governor of Masulipatnam in 1636, eventually amassing a fleet of ten ships. His voyages enjoyed protection from the Dutch, English, and Danes, but they were always in danger of assault by the Portuguese. On May 11, 1652, the French traveler Jean-Baptiste Tavernier sailed from Bandar Abbas to Masulipatnam on a large ship owned by Mir Muhammad that carried more than one hundred Persian and Armenian merchants, a Dutch pilot with his assistant and three gunners, and fifty-five Persian horses. In his *Travels in India* Tavernier noted that the Sultan of Golconda's ship "every year goes to Persia laden with muslins and *chites* or coloured calicoes, the flowered decoration of which is all done by hand,—which makes them more beautiful and more expensive than when it is printed."[19]

Eventually the Masulipatnam trading link to the western Indian Ocean was ended by a combination of political and economic changes that culminated in the Mughal conquest of Golconda in 1687 and the steady encroachment of private European rivals along the eastern coast of India. Furthermore, Golconda shipping had increasingly become victimized by European piracy. In 1665, for example, the sultan's vessel had been seized by the Portuguese on route to Persia, while another Masulipatnam ship was attacked in the Red Sea by a Swedish ship with a Dutch captain. Seen from the perspective of indigenous trading networks, then, the European rivalry for control of Indian Ocean trade that erupted in the seventeenth century was notable mainly for a dramatic increase of maritime violence. A Bengali ballad recalls how "the dreaded Portuguese pirates, the *Harmads*," a word adapted by Bengali speakers from "armada," terrorized coastal shipping, and "plundered the boats and assassinated their crew, and the boatmen and captains of the seaside trembled in fear of the *Harmads*."[20]

Networks linking Gujarati and Persian merchants were not the only ones operating in the Indian Ocean world during this period. The seventeenth century witnessed the rise of an entirely new network of Asian traders—New Julfan Armenians—that owed its existence to the war of 1603–5 between the Sunni Ottoman and Shia Safavid empires. Individual Armenian merchants had traded in the Indian Ocean as early as the twelfth century as far as India and Southeast Asia. In the sixteenth century small Armenian communities existed at Hormuz, Surat, and around Mylapur on the Coromandel coast. In 1605 Safavid Emperor of Persia Shah Abbas forcibly caused the relocation of the large Armenian community of Julfa, which was located in southern Armenia at the contended border between the two competing Muslim empires, to a suburb of the Safavid capital at Esfahan, in central Persia. The Julfan Armenians were deeply involved in the lucrative overland silk trade. After the new community was founded in 1605, it became the hub of a powerful commercial network that stretched out from New Julfa as far east as Manila and as far west to London and Amsterdam.

The Safavid defeat of Portuguese Hormuz and establishment of a Persian port at Bandar Abbas in 1622 opened up the Indian Ocean to the New Julfan Armenians. By the end of the century a network of New Julfan merchant communities was established at all the major Indian ports and several major interior cities. These included Portuguese Goa, French Pondicherry and Chandernagore, near Madras and Calcutta, plus Mughal Saidabad in Bengal. The most important of their settlements was near Hugli, where they were well placed to exploit Bengali sources of raw silk production and the silk trade. In 1688 they signed a treaty with the EIC the purpose of which was to divert the silk trade from its overland route through Ottoman lands to an overseas route to London. To secure Armenian cooperation, the EIC promised the Armenians access to company ships at favorable terms, low custom fees, and "liberty to live in any of the Company's Cities, Garrisons, or Towns in India, and to buy, sell, and purchase Land or Houses, and be capable of all Civil Offices and preferments in the same manner as if they were

Englishmen born, and shall always have the free and undisturbed liberty of the exercise of their Religion."[21] This generous concession facilitated the establishment of New Julfan communities and Armenian churches throughout EIC India. An Armenian merchant further cemented these links by negotiating the EIC lease that created the new company headquarters at Calcutta.

In the 1690s EIC interest in attracting Armenian merchants to Madras went so far as to propose designating that a quarter of the proposed expansion of the city "be set apart for the Armenian Christians to build their new church . . . and convenient dwelling houses for their merchants . . . that quarter so set apart you may call Julpha, that being the town from whence Shah 'Abbas the Great brought them when he conquered Armenia."[22] From Madras Armenians developed their trade in Coromandel cottons and diamonds from Golconda. Madras also afforded them easier access to the ports of the eastern Indian Ocean. In Southeast Asia they established communities in both independent ports of trade and those controlled by the VOC. At the very edge of the Indian Ocean world Armenians pioneered trade to Manila, which was under Spanish rule from 1571.

The success of the New Julfan network depended on several institutions. Literacy facilitated business correspondence and commercial intelligence, which was communicated confidentially through a sophisticated courier system that always brought information back to New Julfa. In this their commercial network mirrored that of other important Indian Ocean merchants. Unique to the New Julfan network in the Indian Ocean context was their adoption of the *commenda* system as part of the Armenian family firms around which trade was organized. The commenda was a legal contract between a merchant with capital or goods and an agent who was willing to work for him on trust. In addition, the system of trust that this system regulated was enforced by a set of community institutions intended to prevent its breakdown. Because everything within the Armenian commercial network ultimately came back to New Julfa, the commenda system provided a built-in check on overly ambitious or simply unscrupulous agents acting against the interests of their sponsors, since the agent's family was an integral member of the very same community. However, this system proved to be limiting because trust was restricted to members of the New Julfan community.

In the end, this remarkable Armenian commercial network collapsed in the mid-eighteenth century under violent circumstances reminiscent of those that gave rise to it almost 150 years previously. First, the 1722 Afghan conquest of Safavid Persia, including the capital Esfahan, signaled an important rupture at the heart of the Armenian network, as did the political chaos of the years immediately following. More significant, extraordinarily heavy taxation imposed in the late 1740s on New Julfa merchants by the founder of the Afsharad dynasty, Nadir Shah, indiscriminate looting by his troops, and arbitrarily administered violence brought the community to its knees and effectively disrupted its network. Even before the worst excesses of 1746–47, a member of the prominent merchant Minasian family wrote to a brother in India, "there is no traffic in trade in our country and day by day [the economy is in ruins]."[23] Combined with the increasingly dominant position of the EIC in India, there was no future left for the once-thriving New Julfan Armenian merchant network in the Indian Ocean.

Each European pretender to Indian Ocean power also created its own network, none more effective than that established by the VOC linking its capital at Batavia with Colombo and Cape Town. Colombo, on the southwest coast of Sri Lanka, represented the midway node between the two extremes of Indonesia and the Cape, while Cape Town acquired the moniker "tavern of the seas" for its role in provisioning VOC ships that made port there, restoring its crews, and being the Dutch link between the Indian and Atlantic Oceans. One aspect of the VOC network that bears witness to the way in which their Indian Ocean posture was developing into a genuinely colonial presence is the way in which the Dutch used the Cape as a place of exile for dissident Indonesians.

The most prominent of hundreds of political exiles from Batavia to the Cape was Shaykh Muhammad Yusuf al-Maqassari, a charismatic Muslim leader from the important city of Makassar, capital of the small state of Gowa on South Sulawesi Island in the eastern reaches of the Indonesian archipelago. Gowa had emerged as an important state only in the early sixteenth century and grew to become the dominant trading port of eastern Indonesia in the seventeenth century by virtue of its rulers establishing a policy of free trade. This policy directly countered VOC ambitions to monopolize the spice trade. When in 1615 the Dutch tried to enforce a monopoly on the spice trade in Maluku and prevent merchants from Makassar trading there, its Sultan Alauddin replied, "God made the land and the sea; the land he divided among men and the sea he gave in common. It has never been heard that anyone should be forbidden to sail the seas."[24] Finally, in 1669 the Dutch settled the matter by smashing the great fortifications at Makassar, which they renamed Fort Rotterdam.

Shaykh Yusuf was born in 1627 during a period when Gowa was experiencing conversion to Islam. He was a member of the royal family of Gowa and raised at court, where he was educated by Arab, Acehnese, and local Muslim teachers. After marriage to the sultan's daughter at age eighteen he studied with an important Sufi leader in Aceh before departing for Mecca and Medina via Gujarat in 1649. In Arabia he studied the teachings of several different Sufi Ways or *turuq* (which developed organizations built around ascetic retreat, participation in ecstatic religious exercises, and veneration of Sufi "saints"), gaining personal prominence and now attracting his own students. Although he was an exceptional individual, the path he followed was along the well-established Islamic network. By the late 1660s his reputation had already reached back to Indonesia and he appears to have been invited to return to the Islamic state of Banten, near Batavia, on Java, around the time that the VOC defeated Gowa and seized Makassar. In the 1670s Banten became a center for political refugees from Makassar, which greatly worried the VOC.

Over the next decade Banten politics deteriorated into a civil war in 1682, with Shaykh Yusuf supporting the old Sultan Ageng against his son, Sultan Haji, whom the Shaykh had taught before the young man had left on pilgrimage. Sultan Ageng surrendered to the Dutch, while Shaykh Yusuf escaped with several thousand followers, apparently hoping to reach Makassar, before he too was captured by the Dutch. Because many regarded Shaykh Yusuf as a saint, the Dutch exiled him to Colombo in 1684; but Ceylon was on the pilgrimage route to the Muslim holy lands and Shaykh Yusuf was unrestricted in his movements and meetings. His notoriety was such that even the Mughal emperor Aurangzeb knew of his exile in Ceylon and asked the Dutch to treat him well. In 1689 the VOC commander at Fort Rotterdam forwarded a request for the return of Shaykh Yusuf to Makassar, declaring in a letter to the Dutch governor-general that "the request had come from the common man, and the masses in Makassar hold this same Syaikh [*sic*] in such great love and awe as though he was a second Muhammad."[25]

Unable to quell the demands for Shaykh Yusuf's return to Batavia nor to curb his influence from exile in Colombo, in 1694 the VOC removed him to the Cape of Good Hope, accompanied by forty-nine family members, slaves, and followers. Because he was from Banten, an independent Muslim sultanate, and not a Dutch subject, at the Cape Shaykh Yusuf continued to enjoy the freedom of movement and association due to a prisoner of state. He died five years later outside Cape Town at the farm on which he was settled, a place that became known as Makassar Downs.

The saga of Shaykh Yusuf demonstrates the imbrication of two quite distinct Indian Ocean networks, the first Islamic and following historic commercial networks linking maritime Southeast Asia to Gujarat and Arabia, the second linking the nodal points of the VOC. However, there is still another layer to his story, one that recalls the pilgrimage of Mir Kamal-al-din from Masulipatnam to Persia to visit the tomb of a Sufi saint. Following Shaykh Yusuf's death, his family finally won the right to return to Makassar in 1705. Shaykh Yusuf was neither the first nor the last political exile from Indonesia by the VOC. Moreover, like the members of his family entourage, some even managed to return to Indonesia, so that the circuit of exile became a two-way network. One consequence of this systematic movement was the implantation of Islam at the Cape, certainly something the VOC had not planned as part of its Indian Ocean policy. In addition, the prominence of visiting *kramats*, or holy tombs, as part of Islamic tradition at the Cape echoes travel around similar Sufi sacred geographies along Indian Ocean shores.

European maritime superiority did not go unchallenged in the early modern period. Along the coast of western India two rival indigenous navies clashed with each other and with the EIC to control coastal shipping. The most successful were the Sidis of Janjira Island, about forty miles south of Mumbai, who had ruled this fortified island since 1618. Descendants of enslaved Africans known as *habshis*, a broad name denoting origins in northeast Africa, the Janjira Sidis traced their Indian roots to military service in the Deccan of southern India.

The most well known of these influential Habshi figures in the political history of the Deccan was Malik Ambar, who was *wazir* and virtual ruler of Ahmadnagar from 1600 to 1626. Probably born in southern Ethiopia and bearing the name Chapu, he was enslaved, driven to the coast, and transported to Mocha. From there he was sold in Baghdad to an insightful merchant who recognized Chapu's intelligence, had him educated, converted to Islam, and renamed him Ambar, the Arabic word for ambergris and a characteristic slave name. His value undoubtedly enhanced, in the early 1570s his owner sold him to Chengiz Khan, himself a Habshi and former slave who was by then *peshwa* of the Sultanate of Ahmadnagar, one of the Bahmani successor-states. Over the next quarter century Malik Ambar rose to prominence as a military leader and savvy political operator, working tirelessly to beat back the encroachment of the Mughal Empire under his contemporary Akbar the Great (r. 1556–1605) into the territory of the Nizam Shahi rulers of Ahmadnagar. Having arranged a marriage between his own daughter and his favored youthful claimant to the Nizam Shahi throne, Malik Ambar's army defeated an invading Mughal force in 1601 and secured the throne for the chosen heir, Murtaza Nizam Shah II. As regent and prime minister, Malik Ambar rearranged the kingdom's revenue system, organized the army to defend against the Mughals, founded a new capital city at Khirki (later Aurangabad) in 1610, and ordered the construction of a sophisticated water supply system to the town. It was he who assigned Janjira Island to the Sidis.

From the great fortress they constructed at Janjira, the Sidis became an important factor in coastal shipping north of Goa up to Bombay, whether serving the Mughals or their own interests. Sidi naval power was challenged by the powerful and ambitious Maratha ruler Shivaji Bhosale, whose army was seizing large chunks of western India from the Mughals. Shivaji commanded a series of small forts along the Konkan coast, as well as a fleet of perhaps several hundred ships. Although Shivaji is remembered as a militant Hindu ruler, in the typical Indian Ocean division of labor his ships were captained by Muslims. His several attempts to assert a naval presence on the coast proved to be disruptive to both the English and Portuguese, who were simultaneously contending with Maratha continental expansion. In the process of beating back the Maratha challenge, the Sidis momentarily shifted their alliance from the Mughals to the EIC, but they remained an independent if steadily less powerful coastal naval force deep into the nineteenth century.

This same period witnessed the rise of a much more successful Indian Ocean rival to European-attempted domination of the open seas and trade networks in the shape of the Yaarubi dynasty of Oman. By the election of a dynamic member of their tribe, Nasir b. Murshid, as Imam, the Yaarubi came to power in the mountainous Omani interior in 1624. Nasir united all of Oman with the shared goal of driving out the Portuguese from their coastal fortresses at Sohar and Masqat. The Omani Arabs seized the former in 1643 and the latter in 1650, a year after Nasir's death. For the next eight decades the Yaarubi waged war against two enemies, Portugal and Persia. Their navy possibly strengthened by Portuguese ships captured at Masqat, they attacked Portuguese strongholds at Bombay in 1661 and 1662, Diu in 1668 and 1674, and Bassein in 1674, as well as the Persian port at Kung in 1670. Responding particularly to requests from various Swahili communities along the East African coast, where they chafed under Portuguese domination, Omani fleets sacked Mombasa in 1661, raided Mozambique Island in 1670, and destroyed the Portuguese outpost at Pate in 1689 before their successful siege of Fort Jesus, Mombasa, that lasted from March 1696 to December 1698.

Although the Portuguese briefly reoccupied Mombasa in 1728–29, the loss of Fort Jesus in 1698 effectively marked the end of their presence on the Swahili coast north of Cape Delgado. The steady loss of other Portuguese outposts on the Indian Ocean littoral had already undermined the reach of the once-powerful Estado da India. When the captaincy of Mozambique was separated from Goa in 1750 and a governor-general appointed to Mozambique in 1752, it marked both the reduction of the Estado to a few places in what was now Portuguese India and shifted the focus of Portuguese imperial interests to East Africa.

The Yaarubi rulers of Oman drew most of their revenue from customs duties levied at their ports, but they also began to expand the date plantations along the Batinah coast of northeastern Oman. The demand for labor created by this agricultural plantation expansion, as well as the maintenance of a standing army by the Imam, were harbingers of increased slave trading to the Gulf from East Africa. Maritime raiding was apparently another source of revenue for Oman, such that Masqat gained a reputation as a pirate's den. In 1705 an Omani attack on an EIC vessel caused one official to write that "Muskat . . . is become a Terror to all the trading people of India," while a company pilot's guide published in 1728 cautioned that "the danger of this port is as much from the Treachery of the Arabs as from the Storms and Rocks of the Coasts; for they are not only Pirates and Thieves, but Cheats in every thing wherein you can deal with them."[26]

By this time, however, internal dissension over election to the Imamate gave rise to civil strife in Oman. In 1749 a new dynasty, the Busaidi, came to power. Under the vigorous leadership of Ahmad b. Said, Oman's place as a mercantile maritime power in the western Indian Ocean steadily grew. One immediate consequence of this political transition was that the Omani Mazrui governor of Mombasa rejected the new Busaidi claimant to authority. According to the anonymous nineteenth-century Swahili *History of Mombasa*, which only exists in Arabic renditions, "When the governor learnt that the Imam Ahmad bin Said had come to power, and that he was not of the family of the Imams, he declared himself ruler of Mombasa and refused to recognize the country as a possession of the Imam, and said: Formerly this Imam was my equal: he has now seized Oman, so I have seized Mombasa."[27] Mombasa's independence would eventually be ended by Oman's imperial expansion into East Africa in the long nineteenth century. From the middle of the eighteenth century, however, it was Great Britain that came to dominate the maritime space of the Indian Ocean as it built an empire based around India that eventually extended from South Africa, through the Gulf, across the Bay of Bengal and Malaya all the way to Hong Kong.

CHAPTER 5

The Long Nineteenth Century

From the beginning of British rule in India, a turning point in history that is usually dated to the English East India Company victory at the Battle of Plassey over the Nawab of Bengal in 1757, Great Britain sought—and fought—to secure the maritime routes of the Indian Ocean in order to protect its commerce and, in time, its expanding empire. In 1892, still several years before he was appointed Viceroy of India, Lord George Curzon blustered, "Without India the British Empire could not exist. The possession of India is the inalienable badge of sovereignty in the eastern hemisphere."[1] Achieving this prize was not a straightforward process. Challenges to British sea power came initially from the French, while slave raiding and piracy were a constant threat to Great Britain's ability to ensure peaceful commercial sea lanes. To achieve its goals, in addition to flexing its naval and military muscle, Britain adopted a strategy that also involved making judicious alliances, surveying the complex coastline of the entire region, and developing key strategic ports through modern civil engineering projects. In the last half of the nineteenth century the industrial capitalism that transformed Great Britain gave rise to both the construction of the Suez Canal and the triumph of steamships over sailing vessels in the open sea.

Finally, the expanding tentacles of empire steadily transformed the Indian Ocean world from its historic foundation in maritime commercial exchange, where production was overwhelmingly still in the hands of indigenous peoples and polities, and focused on its ports of trade, to a new system of land-based colonial occupation and European-controlled plantation production for export. If India was "the brightest jewel in the crown" of the British Empire, then this complex set of factors emanating from British India transformed the Indian Ocean from an "Islamic Sea" into what came to be known popularly as a "British lake."

British naval superiority in the Indian Ocean, arguably dates to Great Britain's defeat of France during the Seven Years War (1756–63), but it was not cemented until their decisive victory over Napoleon. At the end of the eighteenth century, with the defeat of the Netherlands by France in 1795, Great Britain seized upon this enforced alliance between its main European and Indian Ocean rivals to take Cape Town, Ceylon (today Sri Lanka), and Java and Melaka from the Dutch, and the Mascarene Islands of Bourbon (now La Réunion) and Île de France (now Mauritius) from the French. Twenty years later, by 1815, the British controlled the Cape, Ceylon, Melaka, and Mauritius, while Bourbon was returned to France by the Treaty of Paris. Just a few years later, the unauthorized occupation of Singapore by Stamford Raffles in 1819 and its formal possession by the British in 1823 almost immediately reduced the economic significance of both Melaka and Dutch Jakarta.

According to British navigator George Windsor Earl, in 1832 Jakarta "was formerly visited by numbers of large junks from China and Siam, and by prahus from all parts of the Archipelago; but from the establishment of the British settlement at Singapore, the perfect freedom of commerce enjoyed at that place has attracted the greater part of the native trade, while that formerly carried on by junks between Jakarta and China has totally ceased."[2] Thus, two decades into the nineteenth century the basic framework of British domination in the eastern Indian Ocean was established, with the Dutch limited to Indonesia and the French an afterthought.

After dealing with its imperial rivals in the eastern Indian Ocean, the challenge for the British was to suppress both the slave trade, which Great Britain had abolished in 1807, and piracy. The South China Sea had a long history of piracy in which the major political power, the Chinese Empire, initially controlled the definition of who was a pirate. Later, the Portuguese, Dutch, and Spanish were in their turn considered pirates by regional maritime powers. By the time the notorious opium trade from British India to China through the European enclave of Canton at Guangzhou was approaching its height in the early nineteenth century, Qing authorities in South China were equally concerned about Chinese piracy.

A report entitled "A Discussion of the Seaport Situation," written by the knowledgeable governor of Fujian Province, Wang Chih-i, in 1799 included the enlightened observation that piracy was caused by lack of economic opportunity, so that prohibiting sea trade was not a solution to piracy. The most feared Chinese pirate at this time was Cheng Yao-I who was the leader of a major pirate confederacy numbering tens of thousands of members around Canton in the first decade of the nineteenth century. His ships disrupted imperial Chinese control of trade,

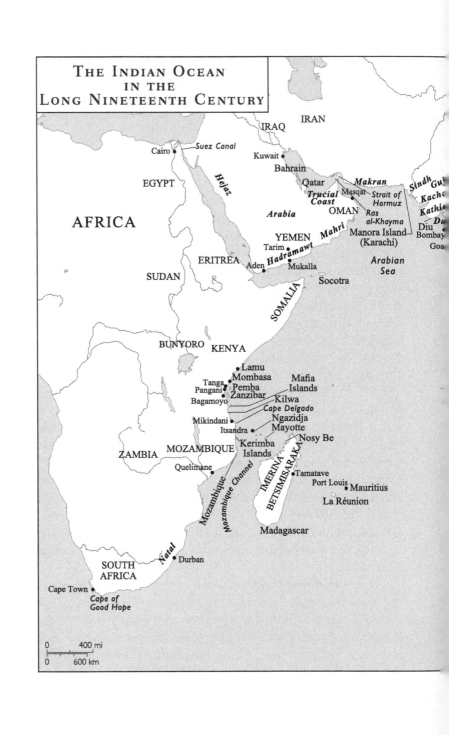

THE INDIAN OCEAN
IN THE
LONG NINETEENTH CENTURY

IRAN

IRAQ

Cairo • ——Suez Canal

Kuwait •

Bahrain

EGYPT

Qatar • *Makran*

Trucial Masqat • *Strait of* *Sindh* *Gu...*
Coast *Hormuz* *Kachc...*

Arabia OMAN Ras *Kathi...*
al-Khayma

AFRICA *Hejaz* Manora Island *Diu* *Da...*
YEMEN *Mahri* (Karachi) Bombay

Tarim • *Hadramawt* Goa

ERITREA Aden • • Mukalla *Arabian*
Sea

SUDAN Socotra

SOMALIA

BUNYORO KENYA

Lamu
• Mombasa
Tanga • Mafia
Pangani • Pemba Islands
• Zanzibar
Bagamoyo • Kilwa
Cape Delgado
Mikindani • Ngazidja
Itsandra Mayotte
Nosy Be
Kerimba
ZAMBIA MOZAMBIQUE Islands
Quelimane •
Tamatave
Port Louis • Mauritius
La Réunion

Mozambique
Mozambique Channel

IMERINA
BETSIMISARAKA

Madagascar

Natal
• Durban

SOUTH
AFRICA

Cape Town •

Cape of
Good Hope

0 ____ 400 mi
0 ____ 600 km

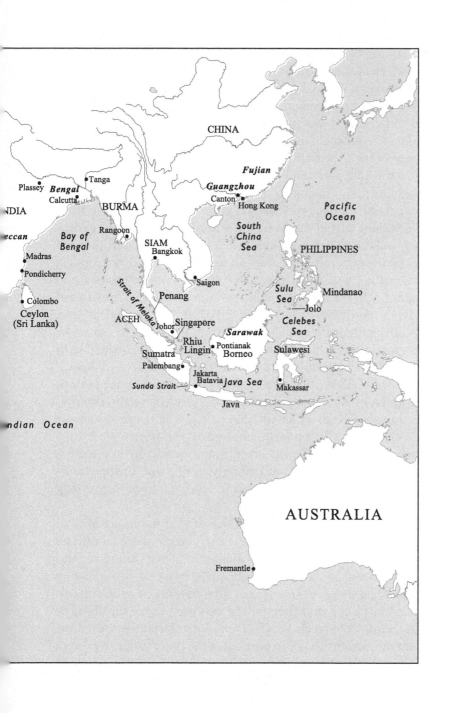

CHINA

Fujian

Plassey •Tanga
Bengal
•Calcutta *Guangzhou*
BURMA •Canton •Hong Kong *Pacific Ocean*

NDIA

eccan •Rangoon *Bay of Bengal* SIAM *South China Sea* PHILIPPINES
•Bangkok

Madras
•Pondicherry •Saigon *Sulu Sea* Mindanao

•Colombo Penang —Jolo
Ceylon (Sri Lanka) *Strait of Melaka* *Celebes Sea*
ACEH •Johor Singapore *Sarawak* Sulawesi
Rhiu •Pontianak
Lingin Borneo
Sumatra
•Palembang Jakarta
Batavia *Java Sea* •Makassar
Sunda Strait —
Java

ndian Ocean

AUSTRALIA

Fremantle •

captured European vessels, and held their passengers and crews for ransom. His activities and those of his widow and successor, Shih Hsiang-ku, eventually forced the Qing dynasty to conclude a truce in 1810 and to grant her immunity from prosecution.

Piracy also reached unprecedented heights in Southeast Asia, where attacks on European and Chinese shipping became indiscriminate. Pirates in the Melaka and Singapore Straits and Java Sea were drawn from several different ethnic groups, particularly the Iranun and Balangingi, and were connected to specific local polities. The center of this system has been called the Sulu Zone, where a maritime state based at Jolo straddled the Sulu and Celebes seas between southwest Mindanao and northeast Borneo. Tracing its roots to 1768, the Sulu Sultanate pursued an aggressive policy of seasonal slave raiding stretching from the Philippines right across the Malay world to provide a labor force for its own production and exchange. Slaves were employed in pearl and *tripang*, or sea cucumber fisheries, in agriculture, and as retainers of every sort, including soldiers, galley slaves, artisans, concubines, and domestic servants. In the eyes of outsiders, Sulu's activities constituted piracy. An 1812 report by J. Hunt, who lived at Jolo for half a year, called the subordinate settlement of Tontoli on the northern shore of Sulawesi, "a great piratical establishment; . . . the town is fortified with 300 guns and 3,000 Illana (Iranun) . . . and 50 or 60 prows."[3] A British observer recorded in 1820, "There are annually fleets of pirate prahus, which come up from Rhio and Lingin, and lie in wait for the defenseless prahus, plundering them of all they possess and murdering or carrying away as slaves all on board."[4] Indeed, as the volume and value of trade moving through the Straits increased dramatically in the nineteenth century, piracy increased accordingly. Moreover, European intervention created a sense of grievance and legitimated piracy among Malay elites.

The British-Dutch Treaty of 1824, which settled the imperial division of maritime space and colonial territory in maritime Southeast Asia, included this critical statement of intent: "Their Britannic and Netherlands Majesties . . . engage to concur effectually in repressing piracy in those seas: they will not grant either asylum or protection to vessels engaged in piracy, and they will in no case permit the ships or merchandise captured by such vessels to be introduced, deposited, or sold in any of their possessions."[5] In particular, the two European powers agreed to eliminate slavery and destroy the markets where pirates sold their captives. Nevertheless, the following decade was the peak period for piracy.

Even with its sail furled, an Illanoan pirate galley was a formidable seaborne vessel, with its armed crew and a cannon mounted at its bow. This particular galley also features a side-mounted steering oar. Charles E. Young Research Library, University of California, Los Angeles

In 1836 a junior British naval officer, Montagu Burrows, bemoaned that the route to China "was more unsafe than ever and piracy more and more organized." Of the pirates themselves he was informed at Penang "about these people, their numerous little squadrons, their well-armed and manned boats (called prahus, pronounced prows) with several guns and well-protected bows, their desperate character, neither giving nor taking quarter, and utter contempt of death."[6] Writing about the British survey voyage of the Indonesian archipelago undertaken by HMS *Fly* in 1842–46, naturalist J. Beete Jukes commented: "Their seas, for the most part so tranquil and easy of navigation, have been left unsurveyed and permitted to swarm with the piratical craft of their own uninstructed chieftains, or those of foreign adventurers who have acquired influence among them."[7]

British interviews with captured Balangingi pirates in 1838 provide some more nuanced insight "about these people." According to a pirate named Silammkoom, who was also an occasional small trader, "Our fleet consisting of six prahus came from Ballongningkin and left that place about 3 months since." The fleet was commanded by a relative of the chief at Ballongningkin who "informed us that the Sultan had desired him to plunder and capture all nations save Europeans. I have never seen the Sultan of Sulu, this is my first voyage to the east coast of the Malayan peninsula, but for many years I have cruised in the vicinity of Manillas, Macassar and other places on which occasion Orang Kaja Kullul [his commander] took any boats he happened to meet."

A second testimony comes from Mah roon, who had himself been captured two years previously and taken to Ballongningkin, "where I was treated as a slave and compelled to perform all kinds of work. . . . I did not voluntarily join the pirates." Echoing the sensitive analysis of Wang Chih-I, a third captive named Daniel testified that "the fact is save 'Mangoorays' (pirating) we have scarcely any other means of getting a livelihood."[8]

Other testimonies reveal in more grisly detail than that of Mah roon the harsh realities of enslavement. A man named Si-Ayer was captured by an Iranun prahu in 1847, where "the prisoners were all kept tied, until they showed no symptoms of attempting to escape; . . . water and rice [were] given to us very sparingly. Some died from hunger, some from being handcuffed, some from grief; they untied me after about a month. If prisoners were sick so they could not pull an oar they were thrown overboard."[9] A decade later Dutch traveler C. Z. Pieters published his experiences as a captive of Balangingi marauders. Upon gaining consciousness, "I found that I was stripped naked and bound in a prahu. . . . The rope at which captives are tied by the neck is taken off in the day-time. At six o'clock in the evening, whether they are inclined to sleep or not, they must lie down and are bound by the feet, hands and neck to the deck of the prahu, and the rope by which their necks are confined remains within reach of the pirates who are keeping watch."[10]

A Spanish captive named Luis Ibañez y Garcia, who was seized at about the same time, remembered with horror that similarly bound captives sat "on the deck of the boat under the scorching heat of the sun, in the rain, and in the winds eye. Some simply collapsed over their oar, dying. Others were untied just on the verge of passing out, in order to regain consciousness, only to be tied up once again on the oar."[11] Enslavement designed to produce still more captives was surely an especially cruel fate to suffer.

As late as 1852, when coal-fueled steamships had just begun to enter Indian Ocean waters, James Brookes, the British governor at Sarawak, on northeastern Borneo, submitted an official memorandum that argued, "It is certain that the extension of commerce depends upon the suppression of Piracy; and it is equally certain that the suppression of Piracy—the extension of Commerce—the success of our settlement of Labuan—the possession of a supply of coal in those distant seas and our national position in the Eastern Archipelago, are but the links of one chain of Policy."[12] No clearer statement of British imperial ambitions could be made. Eventually, with the expanded use and modernization of steamships, piracy was steadily restricted. However, although it only experienced a dramatic decline in the early twentieth century, it was never completely eradicated.

Forging the links of that chain assumed a rather different character in the western Indian Ocean, although the marriage of antislavery and antipiracy prevailed there, as well. The principal challenge to British control of the Arabian Sea came from the Qawasim, an important Arab tribe inhabiting what the British called the "Pirate Coast" who had their main port at Ras al-Khayma, a headland of the Arabian Peninsula that frames one side of the entrance to the Gulf at the Strait of Hormuz. The Qawasim ships ranged from the Gulf to the Makran coast, raiding East India Company vessels and disrupting British designs to expand their control from Bombay into the Gulf. The Qawasim were both opponents of the Omanis for control of the Gulf and allies of the Wahhabis of central Arabia who were challenging Omani control of its inland frontiers.

By the beginning of the century, however, Great Britain had already established itself as a dominating foreign power in Oman by virtue of a 1798 treaty that granted the British the right to build a fortified factory at the Omani capital of Masqat and forbade similar footholds by their French and Dutch rivals. Omani reasons for consenting to this treaty lie primarily in the ruling Busaidi dynasty's interest in protecting their commercial linkages with numerous ports under British domination around the western Indian Ocean. Ratified in 1800, this treaty effectively made Oman the proxy for British imperial designs in the western Indian Ocean.

In this context, British attempts to control Qasimi maritime violence can also be understood as a playing out of the Arab political rivalries in the Gulf. In December 1819 the British seized the Qasimi headquarters at Ras al-Khayma, and in 1820 they imposed a General Treaty of Peace, Article 9 of which joined suppression of piracy with abolition of the slave trade, the major humanitarian and international political campaign of the expanding British Empire, in the following terms: "The carrying off of slaves (men, women, and children) from the coast of Africa or elsewhere, and the transporting them in vessels, is plunder and piracy; and the friendly Arabs shall do nothing of this nature."[13] At the time Great Britain had no interest in obtaining command over the Arabian Peninsula, its chief concern being, as noted by Lord Curzon at the end of the century, "to secure the maritime peace of the Gulf."[14]

By 1853 the British imposed a Perpetual Maritime Truce from which the Trucial Coast, now the United Arab Emirates, took its name. Thus, whether one considers the Qawasim to have been pirates or not, they were certainly political rivals of the Omanis and their British allies.

Again, in 1903 Curzon provided a crystal clear statement that illuminates imperial policy toward this corner of the "British lake" when he explained to a gathering of the sheikhs of Trucial Oman that "the peace of these waters must still be maintained; your independence will continue to be upheld; and the influence of the British government must remain supreme."[15]

The key link between Oman and British India was Bombay, a link forged by Indian merchant capital and the circulation of Indian traders between these two ports. Most of these traders were from different ports in Gujarat and Kachchh; in nineteenth-century parlance they were generally called "Banians," although used in this way the term could sometimes include Muslims, as well as Hindu and Jain baniyas. In the 1760s Danish traveler Carsten Niebuhr reported a population of about 1,200 Banians at Masqat. According to Vincenzo Maurizi, the personal physician of the young Busaidi ruler, Seyyid Said b. Sultan (r. 1804–56), in the first decade of the nineteenth century the population of Masqat had grown to as many as 4,000 Banians among its total population of 60,000. While these figures may be exaggerated, they provide an index to the central financial role played by Gujarati merchants at Masqat throughout the nineteenth century. Arriving at Masqat from Bombay on November 12, 1816, Lieutenant William Heude "saw twenty-five grabs, or small craft, sailing out for Bombay under convoy of the Caroline, an Arab frigate of forty guns. Two other large English-built vessels were in the cove; whilst thirty or forty small craft were loading or unloading their cargoes of dates, salt, rice, and other goods of various kinds."[16]

Gujarati merchants enjoyed a special place in the political economy of an emerging Omani Empire in the western Indian Ocean, while as British-protected subjects they became the advance guard of British imperial presence in both the Gulf and eastern Africa north of the Portuguese possessions. Already by this time Omani customs collection, which was farmed out on five-year contracts to the highest bidder, was in the hands of a Kachchhi Hindu trader named Mowjee Bhimani whose family maintained control of the customs farm at Masqat into the 1840s. No less important was the Shia Muslim Khoja family of Shivji Topan, which was originally based at the port of Mandvi in Kachchh. Omani ruler Seyyid Said was intimately connected to the Shivjis through bonds of friendship and indebtedness, and in 1818 he granted control of the customs farm at Zanzibar to Ebji Shivji. The Zanzibar customs remained almost exclusively in the hands of the Shivji family into the late 1880s.

By the time Seyyid Said followed the logic and encouragement of his Indian trading partners and first visited East Africa in 1826, he had already been obliged by the British to sign an initial antislave trade treaty in 1822. This treaty prohibited trading in slaves to Europeans, empowered British seizures of transgressors, and limited the range of Omani slave trading to a line that ran from Cape Delgado, which marked the nominal boundary between Omani and Portuguese jurisdiction along the East African coast, and extended up to Diu Head on the Kathiawar Peninsula in Gujarat. Following Seyyid Said's defeat of Mazrui Mombasa in 1837, he moved permanently to Zanzibar and made it the Busaidi capital in 1840.

A sign of the further cracking of one of the premodern spice monopolies of the Indian Ocean was the introduction of clove trees to Zanzibar in about 1819. The subsequent development of clove plantations based on slave labor at Zanzibar and Pemba transformed Busaidi Zanzibar from one trading port among many in the Indian Ocean to a major colonial primary crop producer. As a result, antislavery enforcement was difficult and slave trading thrived as the demand for bonded labor spiked at Zanzibar and elsewhere in its coastal East African empire: in the Arabian Gulf where pearl diving and date plantations required a regular supply of unfree labor; and elsewhere in Arabia. Faced with the cozy relationship between Great Britain and the Busaidi dynasty, Captain G. L. Sulivan, commanding HMS *Pantaloon* at Zanzibar in 1866, during the reign of Seyyid Majid b. Said, expressed his frustration in these terms: "In the China seas, should a Chinese junk attack and rob another, we call the crew pirates, attack them, and hand them over to the authorities for execution; yet this infinitely worse piracy is covered by a treaty on the part of a despicable petty Arab chief."[17] In 1873 the British imposed a final antislave trade treaty on Majid's brother and successor, Barghash b. Said. So long as there was demand, of course, slaving continued throughout the nineteenth century, ending only in 1902; while smuggling of individual captives endured so long as slavery enjoyed legal status in Arabia, where slavery was not banned until the second half of the twentieth century.

The experiences of the African victims of the Indian Ocean slave trade merit some reflection here. Thanks to interviews conducted by members of the Royal Navy Antislavery Patrol like Sulivan and the testimonies of Christianized liberated captives there are dozens of such accounts. Most of these come from individuals who were captured as children or young people. Many women were included among the captives. Taken together they reveal the trauma of violent capture in outright raids or kidnapping,

Like the image of a modern soccer team, the crew, interpreter, and thirty-three enslaved Africans sit seriously aboard HMS Racoon for the formal recording of their "liberation." Despite the claims of British abolitionists that the 1873 treaty with the Sultan of Zanzibar effectively ended the slave trade from East Africa, the date of this photograph demonstrates that slave trading died a much slower death. © National Maritime Museum, Greenwich, UK

the deceit involved in the sale of unsuspecting children by older relatives, and the role of debt in pushing people into slavery. Although the oceanic passage from continental Africa or Madagascar to Zanzibar, Arabia, or even the Mascarenes was not as lengthy as the Atlantic Middle Passage—except for the tens of thousands who were shipped on Portuguese and Brazilian ships from coastal Mozambique to Brazil in the first three decades of the nineteenth century—the conditions were just as awful and the effects equally terrifying. Apart from the psychological trauma of being wrenched from one's family and home, as well as the physical conditions of the oceanic passage crammed onboard a dhow, the Arab, Swahili, and Comorian slave traders who dominated the trade further terrified the vulnerable captives by telling them that they would be eaten by white men if they were captured by the British. To take only one example of this cruelty, a Makua boy from northern Mozambique who had been sent in slavery to the Comoros and liberated by a British naval patrol was then shipped on a British steamship to Zanzibar, where he was assigned to the Anglican mission at Kiungani. "In this ship," he wrote, "by which we came we were not at all happy, because some people said to us, 'You are all going to be eaten.' This is why we were unhappy; we did not know they were deceiving us."[18]

With respect to the dhow passage itself, a young Yao girl named Swema who had been marched from northwestern Mozambique to Kilwa in 1865 and whose mother had been killed by her captors on route to the coast, recounted: "Although I was generally indifferent to everything that happened around me, I did not long remain in this state in the dhow, where my suffering redoubled. We were so closely packed that not only could I not turn, but even breathe. The heat and thirst became insufferable, and a great seasickness made my suffering even worse."[19] In the words of another young mission boy from Bunyoro, in western Uganda, whose overland passage to the coast covered more than one thousand miles, until he finally sailed from Tanga, on the northern Mrima coast, with fifty-one other captives:

> We embarked in a dhow with five Arabs and sailed. The first day we
> had bananas to eat, the second day unripe mangoes, and the third day
> the same as the second, both the third and the fourth. Those three days
> there was rain with bursts of sunshine on the sea, but water to drink
> there was not a drop. On the fourth of these days the sea was very
> rough, but we went on till four o'clock, and then we came to Pemba.[20]

Petro Kilekwa, a young Bisa from modern Zambia, who following his liberation by the British in the Gulf first became a sailor and finally an Anglican priest, echoes this account of inadequate food supplies that he and his companions endured as they sailed across the Arabian Sea. Leaving an unnamed port on the Kilwa coast, they were loaded on the lower deck of a large dhow. "We traveled all night and in the morning we found that we were in the midst of the sea and out of sight of land. We went on thus for many days over the sea. At first we had food twice a day, in the morning and in the evening." Their meals often included fish that the Arabs sailing the dhow had caught. "But because the journey was so long the food began to run short and so we were hungry, and also water was short and they began to mix it with salt water."[21] These children and young people grew up into men and women in their many thousands to become the enforced founders of enslaved African-descended communities around the Indian Ocean and into the South Atlantic. Most ended up in Zanzibar, others in Pemba, Kenya, and Somalia, while still others were sent farther overseas to Saudi Arabia,

Yemen, the Arabian Gulf states, Pakistan, India, the Comoros, Madagascar, the Mascarenes, South Africa, and Brazil.

Considering the British obsession with fighting both slaving and piracy, it may seem surprising that the three decades of Betsimisaraka maritime slave raids from eastern Madagascar to the Comoro Islands and coastal East Africa did not provoke a robust British response, although during the era of the raids the British were preoccupied with the oceanic dimensions of the Napoleonic Wars. Reminiscent of the massive raids from Madagascar described 900 years earlier by Buzurg b. Shahriyar, starting in 1785 and not ending until 1816–17 the Betsimisaraka launched a generation of piratical slave raids that terrorized local African populations and the Portuguese colonial authorities at Mozambique Island and the scattered Portuguese northern coastal outposts of the Kerimba Islands.

Raiding parties gathered at the northeast of Madagascar before setting off as a fleet of large outrigger canoes called *laka* for the Comoros. The Betsimisaraka developed special large canoes measuring as much as forty-five feet in length and ten to twelve feet in width for these raids, which were intended to return with captives to be sold off to French traders for the Mascarene sugar plantations. According to contemporary accounts, the largest fleets numbered up to 400–500 canoes with as many as 15,000 to 18,000 men. They utilized prevailing currents and winds, following typical Indian Ocean monsoonal patterns for the raids, which generally occurred on a five-year cycle. The first series of raids were limited to the closer-at-hand Comoro Islands, but eventually the Betsimisaraka were joined by Sakalava canoes from western Madagascar for the raids on coastal East Africa, where they wreaked havoc from the Kerimba Islands as far north as Mikindani, Kilwa, and the Mafia islands. On several occasions these fleets seized and destroyed both French and Portuguese ships in the Mozambique Channel.

Only in 1809 did the British station a ship off the Mozambique coast to provide protection against these Malagasy raiders, although it never engaged them. Eventually, in 1817 the authorities in British India did recommend that the governor of Mauritius take appropriate action, but only after a disastrous final raid put an end to the threat. During this last raid the Malagasy fleet suffered severe losses as a result of storms in the Mozambique Channel, while those who returned carried a virulent strain of smallpox with them. In addition, after they reached the Mafia Islands, the farthest northern penetration of the Malagasy maritime raids, they were pursued and defeated at sea by a fleet of warships dispatched by Seyyid Said, who claimed sovereignty over the southern Swahili coast. Finally, the defeated fleet and the weakened state of the Betsimisaraka were further complicated by the French occupation of Tamatave in 1810. It seems likely that the origins and the legacy of maritime violence that marked Betsimisaraka history in the eighteenth and early nineteenth centuries owed much to the tradition of piracy that was established by their interloping ancestors, for whom this way of life—like that of their Sulu Zone counterparts on the other side of the ocean—provided a means of accumulating wealth to which they would not otherwise have had access.

For a while the British occupation of Mauritius recommended an important relationship with Madagascar, which was a source of both labor and provisions, mainly rice, to the island. But the combination of a difficult relationship with the dominant highland Malagasy kingdom of Imerina and a growing commitment to South Africa, especially following the British occupation of Natal in 1843, meant that Great Britain was happy to leave the southwest Indian Ocean to Portugal and France. Portugal had historic claims to coastal Mozambique, while France still occupied Bourbon and added the small islands of Nosy Be and Mayotte, off the west coast of Madagascar, in the 1840s. Ultimately, France conquered Madagascar in 1895.

The imposition of modern colonial regimes upon the countries of the Indian Ocean rim had a dramatic impact on indigenous societies. Colonialism both expanded the access of Western capital to these areas while restricting it to national businesses. Production and transportation were reorganized for the extraction of colonial primary products, such as sugar, cotton, coffee, tea, and rubber. Christian missionary activity was facilitated and with some exceptions Western education was significantly left to the missionaries.

The European powers imposed new territorial borders that artificially cut through historic or fluid frontiers and frequently divided ethnically discrete societies. A circuit of Indian Ocean shores at the conclusion of World War I reveals that the British Indian Ocean empire—consisting of Crown colonies, protectorates, and League of Nations Mandate territories—included Tanganyika, Zanzibar, Kenya, Somaliland, Sudan, Egypt, Oman, the Trucial States, the sheikdoms of Bahrain, Qatar, and Kuwait, Iraq, Mauritius, India, the Malay States, Singapore, and Hong Kong; France controlled the Comoro Islands, Madagascar, La Réunion, the tiny enclave of Pondicherry on the Coromandel coast of India, and Indochina; Portugal retained Mozambique, Diu, Daman, and Goa in Portuguese India, and East Timor at the far eastern reaches of the Indonesian archipelago; the Netherlands claimed the vast island universe of the Dutch East Indies; latecomer Italy had Somalia and Eritrea. Settler South Africa had gained its independence from Great Britain in 1910, but in every other sense remained a colonial territory. Saudi Arabia, Iran, and Siam were the only significant independent states among those whose coastlines were washed by the Indian Ocean.

By mid-nineteenth century, Great Britain possessed a necklace of critical ports around the greater Indian Ocean littoral from South Africa to southern China. The oldest of these were located in India—most notably Calcutta, Bombay, and Madras; others were added following the British victory during the Napoleonic Wars—Cape Town, mid-ocean Port Louis, Mauritius, and Colombo; while the last lot were acquired to fill in the interstices of the "British lake"—Durban, Aden, Karachi, Singapore, Hong Kong, and Fremantle, in southwestern Australia. Although the ports of the Trucial states, Masqat, and Zanzibar were technically independent, British political domination of all was undoubted, while the final partition of East Africa formally added Zanzibar Town and, more significantly, Mombasa. A few of these ports had natural harbors that could accommodate the rapidly expanding generation of steamships that now plied the waters of the Indian Ocean, but many did not. Modern engineering transformed all of these into modern deep water ports.

Karachi, for example, which the British seized in 1839 and annexed to India in 1843 to become the capital of Sindh Province, appears to have been particularly unsuited for modern shipping, as it was located at the silt-filled delta of the Indus River. In 1841 or 1842 the young Sir Lewis Pelly—newly in the service of British India and serving in Sindh—sailed from Karachi to Bombay in a traditional Sindhi vessel. His boat was anchored at the bar of Manora Island, located to the south of the modern Karachi port and today connected to the mainland by a twelve-kilometer causeway, from which "we proceeded to the muddy shore beyond the city; we were then carried on the backs of some Seedees some two miles to a further boat, which, in turn sailed us to our Dingee."[22] Modern port construction, a railway to the port, and an export-driven agricultural policy transformed what had historically been a minor port into one of British India's main colonial ports. Civil engineering projects at, around, and linking these ports to ever-deepening hinterlands likewise enhanced most of these ports.

Unquestionably, the most significant civil engineering project of the nineteenth century for the entire Indian Ocean was the construction of the Suez Canal. Financed by both British and French capital, dredging of the Suez Isthmus commenced in 1854 and the canal was completed in

More than simply opening up a faster means of travel from Europe to the Indian Ocean, the engineering and dredging of the Suez Canal represented a major achievement of European capitalism and technology. Such imperial exploits were followed avidly in the popular press, as in this illustration from the Illustrated London News, *April 17, 1869.* Courtesy Bodleian Library, University of Oxford

1869. The canal route significantly reduced travel time between Europe and the Indian Ocean world; at the same time the number of ships and volume of shipping expanded exponentially.

Without the invention of steamships, however, this transportation revolution would have been incomplete. Steamships not only enabled Indian Ocean travel to overcome the tyranny that the monsoons imposed on sailing vessels, they also facilitated the expansion of commerce and transformed port hierarchies. The first steamers reached Indian Ocean ports in the 1820s. In 1842 the P&O Company inaugurated steamer service from the Red Sea port of Suez to Aden and the major ports of British India. A decade later the P&O extended its service to Australia. Early coal-powered steamships were neither efficient nor a great improvement on the fastest sailing vessels; later engines generated greater power and were more fuel efficient. But because they did not depend on wind power, steamships provided more predictable service. By midcentury, travel by steamer from England to the Indian Ocean was both faster and less expensive than ever before.

By the end of the nineteenth century, travel time from London to Great Britain's major Indian Ocean ports was cut by more than 40 percent to Kuwait and Bombay, by more than 32 percent to Calcutta, by almost 28 percent to Singapore, and even by some 14 percent to Fremantle. In particular, Aden—blessed with its natural deep water port—and Singapore—with its critical location astride multiple sea lanes—benefited from the increased traffic and the refueling requirements of coal-driven steamships. Initially restricted to carrying passengers and mail, in the long run steamships also became the principal transporters of trade goods. For most of the century, however, both luxury and bulk commodities, as well as people, continued to be carried in sailing ships, both indigenous and Euro-American.

In addition to the goods that had been exchanged for centuries across the Indian Ocean and beyond, the Industrial Revolution created new tastes and a class of the newly rich in Europe and North America who now sought exotic materials from which luxury goods could be manufactured. East African ivory, which because of its whiteness and malleability had been traded to India and China for millennia, now supplied a new market for piano keys, billiard balls, buttons, and combs in the West. The result was the aggressive hunting out of elephants across much of eastern Africa. Rising wealth in the West also created a new demand for pearls, which had for centuries been sourced from beds in the Gulf and off northern Sri Lanka. The consequent need for pearl divers in the Gulf stimulated the slave trade from eastern Africa. In the wake of the coffee craze of the seventeenth century, the habit and fashion of drinking tea created a boom in that trade from China and later from India and Sri Lanka. At the same time, the importation of Western manufactured goods expanded across the Indian Ocean. To take only a single example, until the cotton famine caused by the American civil war, the preferred everyday cloth in eastern Africa became American white sheeting, in Swahili called *merikani*, a name that persisted after the end of that great conflict.

Steam travel made it possible for many more Europeans to travel to and settle around the periphery of the Indian Ocean, although their numbers were minuscule compared to those individuals who were enslaved and transported far beyond their homelands, whether they were African, Malagasy, Indian, Indonesian, Filipino, or Chinese. Furthermore, there were a great many free or uncoerced travelers in the nineteenth-century Indian Ocean. Some were merchants, who like other Indian Ocean peoples before them, established circulating commercial networks that now developed in association with the changing economy of colonial production from West to East. Others were indentured laborers who, though driven by poverty and debt, and sometimes the victims of disguised enslavement, became the main suppliers of plantation labor after the abolition of slavery in the British, Dutch, and French colonial empires. Still others recreated older Islamic networks of scholars and Sufis that stretched right across the Indian Ocean basin. Most of these Indian Ocean nineteenth-century travelers still journeyed on traditional sailing vessels, not steamships, until the 1880s.

Three broad groups of Indian Ocean people were prominent migrants during the nineteenth century: Indians, Chinese, and Hadramis. Of Indians, in general, in the early 1870s Sir Bartle Frere commented, "Along nearly 6,000 miles of sea coast, in Africa and its islands, and nearly the same extent in Asia, the Indian trader is, if not the monopolist, the most influential, permanent, and all-pervading element of the commercial community."[23] In the western Indian Ocean Gujarat was clearly the most important center for the weaving of commercial networks, as it was for textile production. Leading and following the growing colonial presence of Oman in East Africa, Gujarati merchants established themselves in numbers at Mozambique, Zanzibar, northwest Madagascar, and in smaller numbers at the main feeder ports along the Swahili and Somali coast. In the late eighteenth and early decades of the nineteenth century Gujaratis constituted a small, but commercially powerful community at Mozambique of perhaps three hundred men, where they dominated the ivory and textile trades. Ibadi Zanzibar was home to a diverse Indian merchant community of Sunni and Shia Muslims, as well as a small number of Hindus.

From just over 200 individuals in 1819, the Muslim Gujarati community at Zanzibar grew more than tenfold to almost 2,600 in 1874, 86 percent of whom were Shias. Initially an all male population, in the same year 28.6 percent were women and 33.7 percent children. Sent from India to investigate the slave trade in 1873, Sir Bartle Frere was impressed by the industry of Indian men who came to Zanzibar. "Arriving at his future scene of business with little beyond credentials of his fellow caste men, after perhaps a brief apprenticeship in some older firms, he starts a shop of his own with goods advanced on credit by some large house, and after a few years, when he has made a little money, generally returns home to marry, to make fresh business connections, and then comes back to Africa to repeat, on a large scale, the same process."[24]

The most prominent figures belonged to the great trading houses—like that of the Shivji Topan family—with correspondents in Masqat and Gujarat; but by the end of the century the Indian population doubled to more than five thousand and included various artisans, shopkeepers, and clerks. In M. G. Vassanji's historically informed novel *The Gunny Sack*, the story begins by following the route of a character the author calls Dhanji Govindji to Zanzibar in 1885, where he was employed as a clerk before getting established on the mainland at Kilwa. "There were scores of apprentices like himself, from all the villages in Gujharat, Kathiawad, and Cutch it seemed, all lured to the island by dreams of becoming like Amarsi Makan or Jairam Shivji or Ladha Damji—owners of chain stores, underwriters to Arab, Indian and Swahili entrepreneurs, to whom stranded explorers came for credit."[25]

However, not all Indian travelers across the Indian Ocean were traders or aspiring colonists. Abolition of slavery in the British Empire in 1834–35 created a huge demand for labor for the booming plantation production of colonial agricultural products like sugar, cotton, coffee, tea, and rubber. In control of both the supply and demand for labor in their growing Indian Ocean empire, the British developed a carefully monitored system of indentured labor. An interesting precedent to the development of this system was the shipment between 1815 and 1837 of about 1,500 Indian convicts to Mauritius, which became the testing ground for the new system. In India most indentured laborers came from Bengal and Madras Presidencies; in the Indian Ocean world the main receiving territories were Mauritius, Natal, Ceylon, Burma, and Malaya. Following the French abolition of slavery in 1848, the British also permitted some movement of Indian indentured labor to French Réunion, while a smaller number were recruited to East Africa to build the Uganda Railway in the early twentieth century.

Recruitment focused initially on men, but soon women were understood to facilitate a more stable labor force. Contracts generally were for three to five years, but the presence of women gave rise to a permanently settled population. Despite certain similarities to slavery, plus the continued existence of slavery in British India and the fact that a small number of captive Indians had indeed been enslaved in Mauritius, indenture was not slavery. Of the more than 450,000 Indians who arrived as indentured laborers on Mauritius between 1834 and 1910, about one-third returned to India. Nevertheless, the immigration of so many Indians completely transformed the population of Mauritius from being about 80 percent African and Malagasy in the early 1830s to one that was two-thirds Indian by the late 1870s. Of the Indian population, most were Hindu, the remainder being Muslim.

Poverty and lack of economic opportunity drove most men and women to indenture. At first recruitment was individual, recruits coming from among those who had already sought greater opportunity by moving from rural India to cities like Calcutta and Madras. As the system matured, family or clan groups were recruited directly from villages by experienced Indian contract laborers called *sirdars*, who then made the voyage with them to Mauritius and became their representative to their employers and the colonial government. After working in the sugar cane fields of Mauritius for three years, Ramdeen testified to the Calcutta Commission of Enquiry in 1838 that he "was promoted by my master to a sirdarship. . . . My master sent me here with Captain Real to get more Coolies. . . . There are three relatives of mine now with me; if I go I will take them. . . . There are nine of my relatives there now, and therefore I wish to go back."[26] Although conditions could vary during the middle passage from India to Mauritius, the experience was generally better than that for captives in the slave trade, and it improved as the system developed. According to Boodoo Khan, "When I arrived in Calcutta I learnt that I should have to go on board a big ship, and that I was to engage for five years. I did not know how far the island was, or what time would be expended in the passage." His passage to Mauritius involved traveling on two ships on which he perhaps generously averred "we got good food and water, and were well treated" during the two-month voyage.[27]

Women were sometimes subject to abuse by both officers and crew, but for the most part their experience of the middle passage was similar to those of most men. A woman named Bibi Juhooram, who had been unhappy with the way she was treated once she arrived in Mauritius, declared of her six-week voyage from India, "there was plenty of room on board for the Coolies; we had plenty to eat and drink . . . the allowance on board ship was ample."[28] Because these testimonies were given before British authorities in India, they may be unusually positive. Many people did suffer on their passage from India to Mauritius, but overall the oceanic system of transportation was neither as violent nor as deadly as that of the slave trade. Mortality rates to Mauritius from India were less than half those for the nineteenth-century Atlantic slave trade.

Indenture of Indian workers endured as a system to 1938. Several millions of peasants left India as seasonal laborers to work in the coffee

Three indentured south Indian women pick tea on a plantation in Ceylon at the beginning of the twentieth century. Tea picking relied on both female and child labor to select the tender young leaves of the bush. Henry W. Cave, *Golden Tips, A Description of Ceylon and Its Great Tea Industry* (London: Sampson Low, Marston & Co., 1900), courtesy Butler Library, Columbia University in the City of New York

and then tea plantations of Ceylon and the harvesting of rice in Burma (modern Myanmar), while perhaps a quarter million migrated to British Malaya as laborers. South Africa received more than 150,000 Indians, most as indentured workers on the sugar cane plantations of Natal, while a better educated class of so-called passenger Indians because they purchased their own passage also journeyed to Durban from the 1870s. Among this latter group was a young Gujarati lawyer named Mohandas Gandhi, who landed at Durban in 1893, where he developed the practice of Satyagraha, or nonviolent resistance, in 1906 before leaving for England in 1921 and, ultimately, greater fame in India. In each instance these labor-driven imperial connections fostered the evolution of settled Indian communities in these far-flung countries.

The other great movement of indentured laborers was from southern China to Southeast Asia. Bonded labor caused by debt and mostly involving women was historically a major institution in Southeast Asia. In urban areas in Southeast Asia Chinese merchants, like Dutch colonialists, were large slave holders. Abolition notwithstanding, slavery persisted deep into the nineteenth century. The growth of Chinese trade and agricultural production of opium and rice in Southeast Asia during this period created new demands for labor.

In the mid-eighteenth century the junk trade from South China to the countries bordering the southern seas reached its apogee, with more than one hundred junks annually making this voyage. This traffic gradually declined in the following decades as Western shipping sought to gain control of this trade. Yet as late as 1833 a Chinese mandarin named Phan Huy Chu could write as he embarked from Vietnam to Batavia on a Chinese junk, "Every year ships sail to faraway barbarian lands, stable and safe on the waves, as if they were coming and going over flat land."[29] Many of these ships were actually built in Southeast Asia by locally based Chinese shipwrights.

Although this Chinese maritime commercial frontier was already thriving by the end of the eighteenth century, involving Chinese tin miners in Malaya and agricultural workers on Chinese plantations in Singapore and Johor, on the Malay Peninsula, to produce pepper and gambier, the leaves of which were used medicinally in China, it was the rapidly expanding opium trade that propelled it to new prominence. By the 1760s the English East India Company controlled production of opium in India, and British merchants dominated its trade to Southeast Asia and China. From midcentury, Chinese merchants also developed opium farming in Java, eventually expanding right across the entire region. The consequent demand for labor on opium farms, in addition to the other Chinese commercial operations in Southeast Asia, could not be satisfied by local sources and eventually, building on decades of sojourning Chinese labor, gave rise to the introduction of contracted Chinese "coolie" labor. By the late eighteenth century there were numerous settlements of Chinese workers around the Southeast Asian littoral. Opium fueled this entire commercial system, both by driving production and by keeping the immigrant labor force docile.

The negative effects of opium addiction on its people caused the Qing dynasty to attempt to eradicate the opium trade and strictly control European and American merchants at Canton. The First Opium War of 1839–42 between Great Britain and Qing China broke imperial Chinese opposition to the opium trade, led to the British establishment of Hong Kong in 1843, and opened up China to free trade. Henceforth opium came to dominate the revenues of the colonial economies of Southeast Asia. Because of its central location, British Singapore stood at the center of both the opium trade and the immigration of Chinese laborers, while Hong Kong became its counterpart in China. As in India, population growth, poverty, and lack of economic opportunity were the push factors for these migrant workers. In the words of Thomas Church, the Superintendent of Police at Singapore in 1830, "It is, in truth, want and destitution . . . which drive these thousands annually out of China."[30] Nearly all of the Chinese migrants were men until, after 1900, Chinese women began to be able to join men to form families. Even well into the twentieth century, however, the ratio of Chinese men to women in Southeast Asia was significantly skewed. Until the 1870s these men traveled on Chinese junks, but by the next decade they were mainly transported on steamers. Upon leaving China, most contracted debt that continued to bond them to their employers or labor agents in Southeast Asia. Their situation was at best only a step removed from traditional forms of debt slavery in Southeast Asia. By the end of the century, however, about 90 percent paid their own passage.

Singapore was the central clearinghouse for through migration of Chinese, who were contracted out across the entire subregion and across the Indian Ocean to Mauritius, Réunion, and South Africa. Between 1880 and 1910 the annual number of Chinese coolies arriving at Singapore ranged from a low of 50,000 to a high of 200,000.

Already by the 1870s Singapore's population of more than 96,000 included some 54,000 Chinese, of whom fewer than 7,500 were women. It was a diverse Chinese population that included five different ethno-linguistic groups. In addition, Singapore was also home to the so-called Baba or Straits-born Chinese migrants, who had their origins in Melaka and Batavia. The Baba constituted a distinct commercially powerful and wealthy class that actually controlled the coolie trade. The Baba network extended to the most important ports across the entire region, from China to Malaya, even to Rangoon (today Yangon) and Calcutta. According to an anonymous Baba recitation of travel within this commercial network in 1890, the writer first embarked on a small ship from Batavia to Singapore, where he stopped briefly. In his journal he wrote, "I had already come to Singapore sixteen years ago. The city was not as prosperous as it is now. Revisiting the place today things have really changed a lot." Leaving Singapore he then sailed to Saigon (today Ho Chi Minh City) on a larger and faster French steamer, where he stayed with a colleague on "the street of the Babas."[31] In this way were the foundations built for the extraordinary Chinese presence in Southeast Asia today.

The third example of population movement focuses on Islamic networks. Examples of these networks had existed for centuries, but the expansion of the British Empire around the Indian Ocean and the introduction of steamships greatly facilitated movement. Emanating from the Hadramawt and from greater Bombay these new networks carried Sufism and renewed Muslim scholarship across the breadth of the Islamic Indian Ocean. Sufism as a way of worship was organized into specific "Ways" that traced their practices to original founding figures who possessed exceptional spiritual power or *baraka* that was handed down over generations to their most blessed disciples. Each Sufi Way, or *tariqa*, assumed its specific organizational form; these organizations are sometimes known as "brotherhoods." Unlike monastic orders, these organizations were not exclusive, that is, an individual could belong to more than one tariqa, although in practice they could assume fierce rivalries. Among Hadramis the dominant Sufi Way was the Alawiyya, which had reached the Hadramawt from the Maghrib by way of Mecca by the middle of the thirteenth century.

The Hadrami Indian Ocean network dates back to the sixteenth century and reached from the Comoro Islands to western India and the

A group of Hadrami pilgrims from Indonesia photographed at Mecca in the late nineteenth century. Their clothing reflects a combination of Indonesian and Arab styles of dress, but the two umbrellas are clearly of Western manufacture. Tropenmuseum, Amsterdam. Coll. no. 10001261

Deccan, to insular Southeast Asia. Travel and trading were well established among Hadramis, while among Hadrami elites Islamic learning and missionary activity were important activities. The most prominent members of this elite group were identified as *sayyids*, direct descendants of the Prophet Muhammad's son-in-law Ali. Others were regarded as *shaykhs*, religious scholars who did not claim this genealogy. Hadramis came to serve as religious leaders wherever they settled and encouraged the spread of Shafii Islam, reflecting the dominant Islamic school of law in Arabia, around the Indian Ocean. The religious center of the Hadramawt was the city of Tarim, which became a place of return and pilgrimage for Hadramis dispersed in India and Southeast Asia. In a parallel development, as the religious prominence of locally settled Hadrami Sufis grew, their graves also became sites of pilgrimage.

Movement along these elite networks depended on family contacts. An early twentieth-century document written by a member of the prominent al-Kaf family included instructions on how a young man should proceed. Beginning at Tarim it advises the traveler to stay at Mukalla, on the coast of Hadramawt, with a family member "whom we have notified" and who would provide money for further travel. It reminds the inexperienced man to "send presents and letters to your family and children and to us—write from everywhere so that we can rejoice at your well-being." The instructions further recommend, "If there is honey available in al-Mukallā, get some as presents for the relatives in Singapore." Moving next to Aden, where he would similarly be welcomed by family, he should book appropriate passage on a steamer. "Once you arrive in Singapore, follow the advice of your uncle."[32]

The first wave of Hadrami migrants to Southeast Asia dates to the late eighteenth century, individuals moving from Aceh to Palembang and then Pontianak, on the west coast of Borneo. By the 1820s there were important Hadrami trading colonies on the north coast of Java. The 1859 census for Dutch Indonesia counted more than 7,700 Hadramis; by the 1885 census the number had grown to 22,500. By the 1930s perhaps as many as 140,000 people living outside of the Hadramawt could claim Hadrami origins around the Indian Ocean world. Nearly all of the Hadramis who settled in Indonesia were men who married locally; their children were called *muwallads*, a process of family formation that recalls both the formation of Swahili and Mappila societies in an earlier age. Although many Hadramis and Muwallads were simple traders, the high status of some and their first language command of Arabic, the language of the Prophet, gave them prominence in local

Muslim society. Some gained positions within the Dutch colonial enterprise, while others established small, independent sultanates. In 1824, Hadrami sultans were involved in the separation of British Malaya from Dutch Indonesia. From 1873 until 1903 the Hadrami ruler of Aceh, Abd al-Rahman b. Muhammad al-Zahir, led a spirited resistance against the imposition of Dutch colonial rule. By the late nineteenth century a new Hadrami elite based on wealth and education, not ascribed status, emerged. Stimulated by the first stirrings of Indonesian national consciousness and Indonesian Chinese ethnic awareness, they developed a greater sense of Arab ethnic identity. By the 1930s, however, most Muwallads rejected a separate Hadrami identity and sought integration as Indonesians.

On the other side of the Indian Ocean Zanzibar and the Comoros were important nodes of the Hadrami commercial network and Alawi presence. The most important Alawi Sayyid family in East Africa was that of the al-Bin Sumayt, which also had members in Southeast Asia. Among the many distinguished members of this family in the western Indian Ocean, the most prominent was unquestionably Ahmad b. Abi Bakr b. Sumayt, who was born in 1861 on Ngazidja (also known as Grande Comore) at Itsandraa, where his tomb is an important pilgrimage shrine. Ibn Sumayt, as he is known, was a trader, Islamic reformer, and judge, or *qadi*, who gained prominence in British-controlled Busaidi Zanzibar after 1890. In his youth he was also a skilled navigator and astronomer. According to a modern Swahili hagiography, Ibn Sumayt was "a complete dhowmaster."[33] Like other Muwallad—his mother was a member of a prominent non-Sayyid Comorian family—after travel and study in the Hejaz, Ibn Sumayt revisited the Hadramawt, about which he wrote, "Trade is not very developed (in Hadramawt) but its people trade in foreign parts of the world, and for that reason, many people come and go, and eventually they return to their old homelands."[34] Following his first visit to Hadramawt in 1880–81, Ibn Sumayt set out for Zanzibar to serve as a qadi but soon left this position and spent the next several years traveling to and studying in Istanbul, Cairo, Mecca, and Java before returning to Zanzibar in 1888, where he served until his death in 1925.

The Alawiyya was not the only Sufi Way to flourish during this period. By the end of the nineteenth century, eastern Africa was also home to a growing community of followers of the competing Qadiriyya and Shadhiliyya Ways. The Qadiriyya spread from Zanzibar to the coast through Bagamoyo and from there inland along continental caravan routes, while the Shadhiliyya was carried from Ngazidja to Mozambique

Island and then to the interior. Adherents also introduced both independently to Somalia from Arabia.

Beyond the greatly enhanced Sufi networks achieved throughout the Indian Ocean world in the nineteenth century, Sufi saints were considered to be particular protectors of Muslim sea travelers. Coastal shrines dotted the Indian Ocean, while seafarers regularly called upon specific Sufi saints to protect them from the many hazards of sea travel, even after the introduction of steamships. During the stormy passage of Indian pilgrims from Bombay to Mecca in 1903 a female Sufi saint named Baba Jan "saved the steamer from being dashed to pieces after all the passengers, including the European ones, had promised to garland the grave of the Holy Prophet."[35] During the second half of the nineteenth century Bombay, which had become the hub of colonial industrialization and India's major port, had also become a major nodal point for Muslim migration from both its hinterland and foreland, as well as for missionary activities to Iran and South Africa. So while indentured workers and passenger Indians like Gandhi were traveling to Durban, Muslim missionaries carrying Urdu religious tracts published in Bombay followed in their wake.

In addition to the expansion of Sufi Ways, new varieties of popular Islam penetrated the social and cultural practices of most Indian Ocean Muslims. To take only one example, according to an 1869 Alsatian Roman Catholic missionary account a women's healing spirit possession cult at Zanzibar was known by the name *kitimiri*. Identified as an Arab sea spirit, the name of this cult refers to the dog Kitmir who guards the Seven Sleepers of the cave in the eighteenth Surah of the Quran, which is known as the *Surat al-kahf* or "surah of the cave." Part of the elaborate ceremonies surrounding the kitimiri cult involved naming the possessing spirit, who in this case came from Mahri, the country lying between Oman and the Hadramawt, by way of Pemba. In addition, the protective qualities of both the Seven Sleepers and Kitmir were recognized and put into practice as far away as Indonesia. Thus, in their own way the women possessed by kitimiri in nineteenth-century Zanzibar had integrated features deriving from both Omani colonial rule and the Hadrami network.

Another large group of travelers were the sailors who manned the indigenous Indian Ocean sailing vessels, many of whom made the transition to steamships in the lower rungs of the hierarchical order that prevails on board any ocean-going vessel. Most prominent in this motley crew were "lascars," mainly but by no means exclusively Indian seamen who worked on British steamships. An estimate of their numbers in 1855 was about 10,000 to 12,000; by 1881 British merchant ships employed more than 16,600 lascars, a figure that rose to more than 51,600 in 1914. Their work conditions were regulated by a set of Asiatic Articles that amounted to a form of indentured labor distinct from how European sailors were contracted. Another important category of maritime industrial workers were "seedies," African laborers who were often of slave origin or freedmen and who worked mainly as firemen in the suffocating bowels of the ships. So long as the Chinese junk trade continued, of course, their crews were Chinese.

Finally, just as Columbian expansion across the Atlantic introduced deadly new diseases to the Americas with disastrous results, the increased maritime mobility of the nineteenth century was accompanied by the spread of cholera around the Indian Ocean world. Cholera was endemic to Bengal and spread out from there in several devastating epidemic waves in the nineteenth century. The first dated to 1817–22. It ravaged about one-fifth of Bangkok's population in 1820, spreading to Java in 1821, where mortality sometimes reached 60 percent and killed about 125,000. It may also have reached the Gulf and East Africa, as did another outbreak in 1835–37. In 1858 cholera spread from Mecca, where tens of thousands of pilgrims had gathered for the annual hajj, down the towns of the Swahili coast, reaching Zanzibar from Lamu in November.

According to the diary of the British consul at Zanzibar, C. P. Rigby, by February 1, 1859, "the deaths by cholera are reported to be 250 daily. The dead are buried amongst the living, by the roadside in long lines of shallow graves, the earth scarcely covering the toes." Later, in his 1860 report on Zanzibar he summarized the devastation by noting that "in the spring of 1859 it carried off about twenty thousand persons in the Island of Zanzibar, and almost depopulated several towns on the opposite coast," whence it continued south to Kilwa and Mozambique.[36] Experienced explorer Richard Burton was at Kilwa, "where people died like flies," during this horrific epidemic and left this disturbing account of its devastation: "There were hideous sights about Kilwa at that time. Corpses lay in the ravines. . . . The poorer victims were dragged by the leg along the sand, to be thrown into the ebbing waters of the bay; those better off were sewn up in matting, and were carried down like hammocks to the same general depôt. The smooth oily water was dotted with remnants and fragments of humanity. . . . Limbs were scattered in all directions, and heads lay like pebbles upon the beach."[37]

Tents cover the plains outside Mecca where permanent housing for the annual influx of Muslim pilgrims now has been built. This photograph gives some idea of the vast numbers of pilgrims who traveled to Mecca in the late nineteenth century. Courtesy of Rijksmuseum, Amsterdam.

In 1865 another wave of cholera reached Mecca from Singapore and Java, where the epidemic began. That year 15,000 out of 90,000 Muslim pilgrims died at Mecca and from there cholera again spread to eastern Africa, moving first across the Red Sea to Sudan and then up the Nile where it moved along mainland caravan routes right down to the coast at Pangani in October 1869. Eventually the disease killed as many as 30,000 on Zanzibar island. Kilwa Kivinje, the principal mainland port for the slave trade, experienced a daily death rate of 400. In the end cholera extended up the coast to Socotra, down to Quelimane, across to the Comoros and northwest Madagascar.

By the end of the long nineteenth century, Great Britain's colonial enterprise in the Indian Ocean had wrought a whole range of serious consequences that affected millions of inhabitants of the entire region. Some of these were a direct result of the transformations effected by industrialization in the West and the development of colonial plantation production. Others were unintended by-products of the facilitation of population movement. Taken together they accelerated a historical process begun many centuries before that demonstrates how the Indian Ocean world was—more than ever before—both an internally connected world region and one that was globally linked to the rest of the world.

CHAPTER 6

The Last Century

Oil was first discovered in commercial quantities at Well Number One at Masjid e Suleiman in Khuzistan, Persia, in 1908. It was then found at Kirkuk in northern Iraq in 1927, setting off a search for oil reserves elsewhere around the Gulf. On the Arabian side of the Gulf the first oil began to flow at Jebel Dukham in Bahrain in 1932, followed by Dammam on the Gulf coast of Saudi Arabia and the Burgan field at Kuwait in 1938. Although there was no causal relationship between them, the discovery of oil in the Gulf was coterminous with the collapse there of the pearl fishing industry, which was caused by the commercial production of cultured pearls in Japan by Mikimoto Kōkichi. Economic recovery would take years to effect, but oil eventually made it possible for the sheikhdoms to survive and today thrive economically. Oil also dramatically changed the distribution of wealth and affected patterns of labor migration after World War II.

From the beginning, exploration and production of oil were dominated by British and American firms, the appearance of the latter signaling both the increased American presence in global politics after World War II and experience gained in the exploitation of oil in North America. Describing the arrival of the negotiating team for Standard Oil at Jidda in 1933, the distinguished American man of letters Wallace Stegner commented, "They were, without knowing it, [a] social and economic revolution arriving innocently and by invitation, but with implications more potent than if their suitcases had been loaded with bombs."[1] Later in his account of the discovery of oil in eastern Saudi Arabia he wrote of the pioneering days around al-Hasa of the mid-1930s, "the coastal region was a frontier that changed with a magical swiftness once the Americans began to impose upon it the full range of their control over physical nature."[2] Indeed, the discovery of oil marks the most significant development of the twentieth century in the Indian Ocean world, and oil continues to dominate global concerns across the region to the present.

Arab workers operate a drill bit at a well site in Kuwait around 1950. The discovery and exploitation of Arabian oil reserves transformed labor and society in the Gulf and wider Indian Ocean world. Photo by Francis Hadden Andrus

Five other major themes dominate the century after the end of World War I in the Indian Ocean, yet all can be linked to oil in one way or another: the impact of travel by air; the continued expansion of Islam and changes within the faith; the increased threat to human society posed by natural disaster and environmental change; the resurgence of piracy in the late twentieth century; and the renewed geopolitical significance of the Indian Ocean. In some cases these themes reflect a major departure from the earlier themes that dominated Indian Ocean history; in others, they represent the persistence of issues that were sometimes less clearly glimpsed before the twentieth century. All five, plus oil, however, have salience for the contemporary Indian Ocean.

The new configuration of colonial territorial boundaries after World War I had the double effect of more closely linking the fates of those areas under a particular colonial regime, while again redefining the political boundaries of the Indian Ocean. One by-product of this process was the emergence of modern nationalism, the driving force that led to the gaining of independence for the colonial territories. The Japanese invasion and brief, but brutal, occupation of Southeast Asia reinforced these movements in those territories. The different struggles to gain independence among Indian Ocean territories were rooted in variously

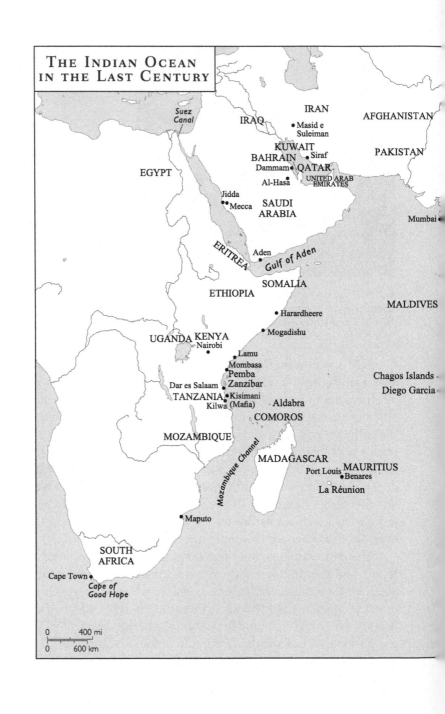

THE INDIAN OCEAN
IN THE LAST CENTURY

Suez
Canal

IRAQ

IRAN

AFGHANISTAN

• Masid e
Suleiman

KUWAIT

BAHRAIN   • Siraf

PAKISTAN

Dammam• QATAR

EGYPT

Al-Hasa•

UNITED ARAB
EMIRATES

Mumbai •

Jidda
••Mecca

SAUDI
ARABIA

ERITREA

Aden
•

Gulf of Aden

SOMALIA

ETHIOPIA

MALDIVES

• Harardheere

• Mogadishu

UGANDA KENYA
Nairobi
•

• Lamu

Mombasa

Pemba

Dar es Salaam Zanzibar

Chagos Islands •

Diego Garcia •

TANZANIA •Kisimani
Kilwa (Mafia)

• Aldabra

COMOROS

MOZAMBIQUE

Mozambique Channel

MADAGASCAR

MAURITIUS
Port Louis •Benares

La Réunion

• Maputo

SOUTH
AFRICA

Cape Town •

Cape of
Good Hope

0   400 mi

0   600 km

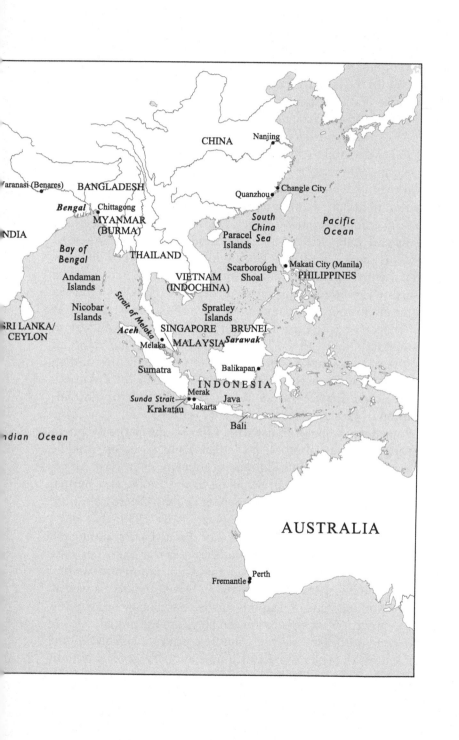

CHINA   Nanjing

Varanasi (Benares)   BANGLADESH   Quanzhou Changle City

Bengal   Chittagong
MYANMAR   South
(BURMA)   China   Pacific
Paracel   Sea   Ocean
Islands

INDIA   Bay of   THAILAND
Bengal   Scarborough   Makati City (Manila)
Andaman   VIETNAM   Shoal   PHILIPPINES
Islands   (INDOCHINA)

Nicobar   Spratley
Islands   Islands
SRI LANKA/   Aceh   SINGAPORE   BRUNEI
CEYLON   Melaka   MALAYSIA Sarawak

Sumatra   Balikapan

INDONESIA

Merak   Java
Sunda Strait
Krakatau   Jakarta

Bali

Indian Ocean

AUSTRALIA

Perth
Fremantle

expressed nationalist visions to overthrow the constraints of colonial rule. In general, as well as in some quite specific instances, the independence of one influenced the continuing struggle of another. The reassertion of Egyptian independence in 1922 had repercussions among all the Muslim societies of the Indian Ocean, as did the post–World War II independence of India and Pakistan in 1947. The violence that accompanied the division of India from Pakistan in 1947 and then of Bangladesh from Pakistan in 1971; Indochina from France in 1954; Kenya from Great Britain in 1963; Mozambique from Portugal in 1975; and South Africa from apartheid in 1994 was driven by factors specific to the character of each colonial regime, while the aftermath of each continues to play out in the postcolonial Indian Ocean world.

Nationalism emphasized the forging of national identity over ethnic particularisms and state citizenship in opposition to the foreignness of noncitizens. This tendency often clashed with the creation of different transnational identities, whether pan-Islamic, pan-Indian, pan-Arab, or pan-Chinese. For example, in the 1930s most Muwallads in Indonesia sought greater integration by accepting local over Hadrami identity. At independence most accepted Indonesian citizenship. Still, elsewhere in the postcolonial Indian Ocean world members of the far-flung Hadrami diaspora were not welcome. An example of how some historic Indian Ocean population movements reverberated violently in the twentieth century was the targeting of Arabs and Indians at the time of the Zanzibar Revolution in January 1964.

The continued migration of Indians and Chinese during the twentieth century, in particular, created problems. Indians came to occupy middle strata between British rulers and indigenous populations in East Africa, where they numbered perhaps half a million in the 1960s, and Burma, where after the mid-1880s they came to represent almost 7 percent—more than one million people—of the total population by 1930, that often caused them to be the most immediate target of dissatisfaction during the colonial era. The Chinese population of Southeast Asia now numbers more than twenty million people. Among their ranks are numerous wealthy merchants, small shopkeepers, professionals, and civil servants, as well as many who are working class. Singapore stands apart for being majority Chinese, three-quarters of its population claiming Chinese origins.

Elsewhere in Southeast Asia the Chinese constitute sizable minorities: 35 percent of Malaysians are of Chinese ancestry, several million Chinese live in Thailand and Indonesia, while many of the largest cities have major Chinese populations. These immigrant populations and the conspicuous roles they occupied in the colonial economy eventually led to scapegoating of these communities for not being indigenous or not having made a full commitment to the new postcolonial nations in which they resided. As early as the 1930s, spurred by Thai nationalism, anti-Chinese measures were adopted by Siam, while anti-Chinese violence erupted in Indonesia in both the 1970s and 1990s. In the 1930s anti-Indian riots, targeted mainly at Muslims, swept colonial Burma, while many Indians fled during the Japanese occupation during World War II. In the 1960s official discrimination caused some 300,000 Indians to leave Burma, while violence against Muslim Indians, who are known in Myanmar as Rohingyas, caused expulsions in 1978, 1991, and has raged as recently as 2012. Exploiting popular resentment against Indians in Uganda, in 1972 Idi Amin ordered the expulsion of all South Asians in ninety days.

The definition of modern state borders also had the effect of redefining the terms of travel in the Indian Ocean. For millennia travel by sea was generally unrestricted or only partially controlled, the attempts to control maritime travel by the early modern European colonial regimes notwithstanding. Colonialism now marked the native peoples of the Indian Ocean region as subjects—not citizens—of one colonial power or another; and while borders were definitely porous, seaborne travel was increasingly subject to the possession of a passport or its official equivalent even as movement at the local level still operated as a function of family, village, or communal affiliations. Other continuities persisted, as well, such as the role of smaller indigenous sailing and then motorized craft to fill in the maritime interstices to which steamships were unable to gain access because of their deep draft and overall size and to carry materials that were not economical for steamships to transport, like mangrove poles by dhow from the Swahili coast to Arabia. Here is where the transportation revolution comes into play, as most travelers and sojourning workers today travel by air, rather than by ship. To be sure, the petrochemical industry soon made coal-powered ships obsolete and made possible more efficient engines. Improved engine design also boosted the power of steamships. Without a doubt, modern steamships enhanced oceanic travel by linking the ports and hinterlands of the Indian Ocean shores. For most Euro-American travelers steamers could provide a respite from daily cares. Steaming from Ceylon to Mauritius in April 1896, Mark Twain wrote,

> We are far abroad upon the smooth waters of the Indian Ocean, now; it is shady and pleasant and peaceful under the vast spread of the awnings, and life is perfect again—ideal. . . . There is no mail to read

and answer; no newspapers to excite you; no telegrams to fret you or fright you—the world is far, far away; it has ceased to exist for you— seemed a fading dream, along in the first days; has dissolved to an unreality now; it is gone from your mind with all its businesses and ambitions, its prosperities and disasters, its exultations and despairs, its joys and griefs and cares and worries. . . . This sort of sea life is charged with an indestructible charm. There is no weariness, no fatigue, no worry, no responsibility, no work, no depression of spirits. There is nothing like this serenity, this comfort, this peace, this deep contentment, to be found anywhere on land. If I had my way I would sail on for ever and never go to live on the solid ground again.[3]

But in the last decades of the twentieth century air travel eclipsed sea travel as a means to move people around. It also removed the experience of the ocean from traveling across the vast spaces of the Indian Ocean. Concomitant advances in naval design eventually produced the giant container carriers that today dominate global commercial shipping. Changes in technology have also significantly reduced crew size on these ever larger ships, while the crews themselves have become increasingly diverse and unconnected to both the flag registration and home ports of shipping.

The oil industry initially depended exclusively on foreign capital, management, and labor. Educating local men to work as skilled labor in the industry and regional political leaders to support the development of modernized states was one aspect of how oil transformed the Gulf states, including Saudi Arabia. By the last decade of the twentieth century, the combined nationalization and globalization of oil production in Saudi Arabia yielded a labor force that was almost three-quarters Saudi and less than 6 percent American, with the remaining roughly 21 percent including employees from more than forty countries. A different demographic impact can be seen in Kuwait, Bahrain, Qatar, and the United Arab Emirates (UAE), where the wealth produced by oil has caused a massive immigration of foreign residents to support burgeoning urbanization.

While there are many well-heeled Westerners and Asian businessmen who now reside in these cities, the working class is mainly from other Arab countries, South Asia, and the Philippines. In 2010 the UAE population was composed of 11.5 percent Emirate citizens and 89.5 percent foreigners, with a more than 2:1 male to female ratio; for Qatar the data show that only 15 percent are citizens of the Sultanate, 13 percent other Arabs, and 72 percent non-Arab foreigners, while the male to female ratio is 3:1. Comparable data for Kuwait and Bahrain are less dramatic, but taken as a whole the skewed demography of the Gulf emirates reflects both the realities of the contemporary global labor market and the great disparities of wealth among nations. Such gender disparities recall certain characteristics of the earlier era of indentured labor, which can be regarded as a bridge between slavery and a "free" labor market in the Indian Ocean world.

Air travel has also had its effect on the movement of millions of Muslim pilgrims during the annual hajj season to Mecca. Jidda is still the port of entry for pilgrims, but it is now the Hajj Terminal at King Abdulaziz International Airport north of Jidda that serves as the principal terminus for pilgrims traveling to the Holy Lands of Islam. In addition to facilitating the annual mass of modern pilgrims, during the late colonial period, as part of their efforts to recruit Muslims to oppose insurgent nationalism, the Portuguese rulers of Mozambique courted favored Muslims by offering them free air passage from Lourenço Marques (now Maputo) to Arabia so that they could complete the hajj. Air travel has similarly facilitated the movement of Muslim missionaries from the Middle East and South Asia to Africa and Southeast Asia, as it has also connected Hindu emissaries to Mauritius and South Africa. One important impact of such easy movement of individuals and ideas has been the broad dissemination of different reformist and revivalist movements across the Indian Ocean world. The influence of Salafism, the literalist and puritanical version of Sunni Islam that prevails in Saudi Arabia, was also facilitated by the enormous wealth created by oil in Saudi Arabia, which constructed Arabian-style Friday mosques in as many Indian Ocean Muslim communities as possible. Such Islamic ideologies have regularly opposed both the earlier Sufism that spread widely during the nineteenth century and the broad range of popular practices that had their origin in the adaptation and integration of Islam in places as distant from each other as the Comoros and Indonesia.

Radical notions of religious orthodoxy, including those implanted by Christian missionaries and their indigenous adherents, have affected both communal relations and global politics in many parts of the Indian Ocean world. Those that can be attributed to modern travel as well as modern communications—including newspapers, radio, television, and the Internet—include the spread of militant Hinduism from India to Mauritius and consequent tensions with the Mauritian Muslim community, who ironically share South Asian roots. Better known are the al-Qaeda attacks against American embassies in Nairobi and Dar es Salaam in 1998; the Lashkar-e-Taiba attack on Mumbai in 2008, carried out by militants arriving by inflatable speedboats from

Pakistan; and the 2002 car bombing in Bali and the 2009 hotel bombings in Jakarta organized by al-Qaeda-linked Jemaah Islamiyya. A vivid illustration of the link between the securing of oil sources, maritime geopolitics, and radical Islam is the speedboat bombing carried out in 2000 by al-Qaeda against the USS destroyer *Cole*, which was harbored at Aden as part of the United States Seventh Fleet committed to the Gulf wars.

Environmental change, global warming, and natural disasters constitute a third major theme engaging the Indian Ocean world in the modern era. Natural disasters are, of course, not exclusive to the history of the last century, for example, the earthquake that leveled the Persian port of Siraf in 977. Because of the well-established connection between climatic fluctuations and major outbreaks of disease, disturbances in the Asian monsoon dated to 1816 are regarded as one of the causes of the first great Bengal cholera epidemic. On the other side of the Indian subcontinent, the dreadful famine of 1817 may have been a factor in pushing many Indian merchants farther afield in the western Indian Ocean. A freak hurricane that struck Zanzibar in 1872 destroyed property and wiped out the entire clove crop. Assaying the damage inflicted on the British Consulate, Sir John Kirk wrote, "As the sea rose, sheets of salt spray and rain drifted in at the broken windows and filled the rooms a foot with water. . . . The sea was driven with such force as to undermine and sweep away the whole embankment of stone and double row of wooden piles that protect the foundations of the English, German and American consulates."[4] Ironically, the aftermath of this particular natural disaster opened up Pemba Island, which was largely spared by the tempest, to greatly increased clove production.

Although cyclones are unusual as far north as Zanzibar, they are a regular feature of the southern Indian Ocean. Both Mauritius and Réunion have suffered more than once as a result of their enormous power, while on some occasions they have swept across Madagascar and the Mozambique Channel to cause extensive flooding along the Mozambique coast, where these storms are known as *monomocáias* and occur during the transition between monsoons. Such storms visited Mozambique Island in 1841–43, when "ships were unfastened from their moorings and grounded," and relatively late in 1858, when a variety of local, Arab, and French vessels "were flung on the beach."[5] More recently, in 2000, Hurricane Hudah caused extensive damage across both Madagascar and Mozambique, displacing hundreds of thousand of people from their homes.

The worst hit area of the storm-driven disasters historically has been the low-lying flats of the northern Bay of Bengal, for which storm records date back to the late sixteenth century. In the last half-century, horrific human losses have resulted from the 1970 Bhola Cyclone that took more than half a million lives in Bangladesh; the 1991 cyclone in which some 143,000 lives were lost and ten million people made homeless in Chittagong; and the 2007 Cyclone Sidr, which left a million homeless and killed more than 3,000 people. The following year Cyclone Nargis killed another 140,000 people along the coastline of the eastern Bay of Bengal, hitting Myanmar, where it made landfall, especially hard.

The most widely known modern natural disasters of the Indian Ocean have been caused by volcanic activity along the Indonesian edge of the Pacific Ring of Fire. Lying in the Sunda Strait between Sumatra and Java, Krakatau exploded in 1883, killing nearly 36,500 people according to Dutch records and possibly uncounted thousands more. The town of Merak on Java was inundated by a 150-foot-high tsunami. The effects of what has been described as the loudest noise ever heard in world history were global. Because of the cloud cover created by volcanic ash, for a year after the eruption global temperatures lowered by up to 1.2°C, temperatures did not return to normal for five years, and weather patterns were disrupted. Lava rafts, some with human skeletons, drifted as far west as the coast of eastern Africa. More recently, the devastating tsunami that was caused by a volcanic explosion off the northwestern coast of Sumatra in December 2004 affected the coast from Sumatra to Thailand to Sri Lanka to Tanzania. As is well known, it caused huge population loss of more than 230,000 and displacement in fourteen countries, as well as deep emotional scarring. The televising of images from around the Indian Ocean made this natural disaster a truly global event. Undersea volcanic activity off the same coast continues to plague northern Sumatra with earthquakes always posing a threat of tsunamis.

Unrelated to volcanic activity but equally worrying is the rise of sea levels in the Indian Ocean as a consequence of global warming. Here the example of the ruins of the medieval town of Kisimani, located on a peninsula on the southeastern coast of Mafia Island to the north of Kilwa, on the Swahili coast, is fascinating. Kisimani had been attacked in 1816 by Sakalava raiders, but according to a version of the history of a neighboring village recited in 1955 by Shaykh Mwinchande b. Juma, "Kisimani was not destroyed by war but by the rising of the sea. Kisimani was a large town. . . . But because of the water there is no one now who knows where it was."[6]

Similar examples certainly exist for other Indian Ocean coastal locations, as long-term changes in the world's climate have affected sea levels. More threatening today, however, is the compounding of natural

These fishing boats sit among the wreckage of an Indonesian community on Sumatra, near the epicenter of the 9.0 earthquake that triggered the tsunami. The terrible power of the 2004 Asian tsunami destroyed coastal settlements from Indonesia to East Africa. UNESCO Image

climatic fluctuations with global warming caused by the use of fossil fuels and other human impacts on the natural environment. The tiny, low-profile Andaman and Nicobar islands at the south end of the Bay of Bengal, which suffered great human losses in the 2004 tsunami, and the Maldive Islands in the Arabian Sea are now threatened with being slowly inundated, as are similarly vulnerable coastal zones.

Although piracy has never entirely disappeared in the past century, from the late twentieth century this form of maritime violence experienced a resurgence in the Straits of Melaka and Singapore. Much of this activity has been characterized by the opportunistic, hit-and-run actions of desperate fishermen whose livelihoods have been negatively affected by commercial overfishing. The amazing growth of the volume of container shipping passing through this critical sea lane has also attracted its share of organized criminal piracy. Today Singapore is the largest container port in the world. An unanticipated consequence of the development of container ships is that they are easier to attack because of their huge size, small crews, and perpendicular hulls, which make them easier to scale using grapples thrown over a ship's gunwales from attacking speed boats.

Oil tankers are another potentially rich target of pirates. According to research conducted by Australian security scholar Carolin Liss, "These attacks are characterised by a high degree of organisation and require detailed planning and upfront capital. An example is the shipjacking of the tanker Selayang on 20 June 2001 in the Malacca Straits by 19 pirates. The vessel had a tracking device on board and the Indonesian authorities were able to arrest the hijacked ship and some of the pirates on the 27th of June near Balikpapan. According to the pirate's statements, they had been hired to conduct the attack by a man called Mr. Ching, who had only limited contact with the perpetrators and remained anonymous."[7] Although piracy still persists in maritime Southeast Asia, since about 2000 the focus of Indian Ocean piracy has been Somalia.

The collapse of the Somali state in 1991 and the consequent inability to protect the coastal waters of northern Somalia from foreign commercial fishing vessels has resulted in severe overfishing of these waters. In addition, both European and Asian shipping have dumped toxic chemical waste in Somali coastal waters, which further devastates the fishing beds. Deprived of their livelihood, the Somali pirates were first drawn from the ranks of local Somali fishermen. According to maritime security analysts Michael Frodl and John Manoyan of the National Defense Industrial Association, this first generation of modern Somali pirates "consists of largely opportunistic pirating within 50 miles of Somali shores, especially in the Gulf of Aden, which has occurred for centuries."[8] One of the leaders of these pirates, named Sugule Ali, told a reporter for the *Independent* (London) in January 2009, "We don't consider ourselves sea bandits. We consider sea bandits (to be) those who illegally fish and dump in our seas."[9]

After a decade of activity in the Gulf of Aden, Somali piracy eventually forced its way into global consciousness in 2008 after the seizure of a French luxury yacht and the payment of a huge ransom to release its crew. Following several other dramatic attacks, in April 2009, four Somali pirates seized the United States flagged MV *Maersk Alabama*. When fears for the safety of its American captain grew, US Navy SEAL snipers killed three of the four pirates and the fourth surrendered. Spectacular cases like these drew wide international attention to Somali piracy. Emboldened by the success of some of these daring attacks, Somali piracy grew exponentially in the next several years, including the hijacking of the Saudi oil tanker *Al Nisr Al Saudi* in 2010. The small coastal town of Haradheere, located about 250 miles northeast from Mogadishu, has gained a reputation as a major center for piracy. This once obscure place was described by a Reuters journalist in December 2009 as "a bustling town where luxury 4x4 cars owned by the pirates and those who bankroll them create honking traffic jams along its

*A crew from the European Union Naval Force Somalia (Operation Atalanata)
captures a boatload of would-be Somali pirates on March 4, 2009. By 2012
political changes in Somalia and Somaliland plus the combined maritime efforts
of many nations had severely reduced the chaos caused by Somali pirates.*
Photographic service of the Council of the EU, © European Union

pot-holed, dusty streets." According to what he was told by Mohamed
Adan, deputy security officer for the town, "Piracy-related business has
become the main profitable economic activity in our area and as locals
we depend on their output."[10]

Especially worrying for every nation with economic and strategic
interests in the western Indian Ocean, Somali piracy soon extended as
far south as the northern end of the Mozambique Channel and as far
east as a few hundred miles from Mumbai. Its activities precipitated
increased maritime security practices, stepped up international naval
operations and the arming of many merchant marine vessels, and encouraged local counterpiracy efforts in a combined effort to eliminate
this threat to Indian Ocean shipping. Whatever the future of piracy in
the Indian Ocean there can be no doubting that it has been a feature of
its maritime history for at least two millennia.

Whether in the western Indian Ocean or in Southeast Asia the suppression of piracy is clearly a concern of regional nation-states, global
powers with strategic interests in the region, and international business.
Just as Great Britain regarded Mauritius to be strategically significant in
the early decades of the nineteenth century, islands have occupied an

important place in the recent geopolitics of the wider Indian Ocean. After World War II the United States moved to contain what it believed to be the Soviet threat in the Indian Ocean. This Great Power competition played itself out in many places, from Ethiopia and Somalia in the 1970s to Afghanistan in the 1980s.

However, the most striking example of how big power manipulations have affected the people inhabiting the smallest islands of the Indian Ocean is the case of Diego Garcia, a coral atoll with an entrance channel on its northern side. The United States initially explored the establishment of a secure base from which to operate in the 1960s. The first candidate was uninhabited Aldabra Island, a British possession located to the north of Madagascar, but the British refused because it was and remains a protected breeding ground for rare giant tortoises. Instead, secret negotiations were carried out between the two allies to give the United States rights over tiny Diego Garcia, the largest island of the Chagos archipelago just south of the Maldives and south of the Equator. In exchange for the United States underwriting research and development costs for the British acquisition of Polaris missiles, the United Kingdom leased Diego Garcia to the United States for ninety-nine years without reference either to Parliament or Congress.

In 1971 the United States began construction of a naval communication facility on Diego Garcia, upgrading it in 1977 to a complete military support facility. The Iranian Revolution in 1979 accelerated expansion of the base and, at a cost of half a billion dollars the full naval base was completed in 1986. It played a major air and naval support role during the first Gulf War, as well as during the second Gulf War. Whether the justification for these wars was to secure Middle Eastern oil or to fight against Islamic terrorism, the price paid by the people of the Chagos Islands was steep.

The islands had been a dependency of British Mauritius since 1814. Their tiny population was the descendants of enslaved Africans who had been landed there to work on coconut plantations. As a precondition to Mauritian independence in 1967 the Chagos were removed from Mauritian jurisdiction in 1965 and renamed the British Indian Ocean Territory. Between 1967 and 1973 all the Chagossians, perhaps as many as 2,000 individuals, were forcibly removed from the islands and relocated to Mauritius, about 1,200 miles away, where today they are an impoverished and somewhat despised urban enclave in Port Louis simply called "Ilois," or islanders.

Finally, in 2000 the Chagossians won a British court decision that allowed them to return home, but it was blocked by the Labour

Government of Prime Minister Tony Blair. Three years later a British court denied them monetary compensation. On May 12, 2006, as it ruled in their favor to return home, the British High Court delivered this scathing judgment: "The suggestion that a minister can, through the means of an order in council, exile a whole population from a British Overseas Territory and claim that he is doing so for the 'peace, order and good government' of the territory is to us repugnant."[11] Repugnant or not, the House of Lords rejected the claims of the Chagossians and they remain exiled today.

Although many of the original exiles have died, others and their children persist in the struggle to claim their ancestral rights. In the words of Chagossian community activist Louis Olivier Bancoult, "We are reclaiming our rights, our rights like every other human being who lives on the Earth has rights. . . . I was born on that land, my umbilical cord is buried on that land, I have a right to live on that land. It cannot be that a foreigner profits from all my wealth, profits from my sea, profits from my beaches, profits from my coconuts, profits from it all, while I'm left with nothing." The Chagossians, he told his interviewer, are "asking for our islands, our fundamental rights, and our dignity."[12]

Far to the eastern reaches of the Indian Ocean, a more recent struggle has focused on the South China Sea, where China, Vietnam, the Philippines, Malaysia, and Brunei have forwarded overlapping claims to the Spratly and Paracel islands and the Scarborough Shoal. In differing combinations these sovereign nations seek to control potential undersea hydrocarbon reserves and fisheries beyond their internationally recognized coastal zones. Another aspect of Chinese claims concerns freedom of navigation through the South China Sea, through which fully one-third of global shipping passes. While China asserts it is part of their territorial waters by right of deep historical connections, the United States counters that it has been historically and must continue to be regarded as being in international waters. The naval presence of these global rivals is also complicated by the 1951 mutual defense treaty between the United States and the Philippines. In April 2012 China and the Philippines carefully stepped back from a potential armed confrontation over possession of the disputed Scarborough Shoal. Meanwhile, the potential for future conflict looms over this critical body of water, where "there are regular maritime clashes between fishermen, oil exploration ships and naval or coastguard vessels as the claimants refuse to concede ground."[13]

More hopefully, the creation of an Indian Ocean Rim Association for Regional Cooperation (IOR-ARC) was suggested in 1995 by then-president Nelson Mandela of South Africa, during a visit to India, who declared that "the natural urge of the facts of history and geography . . . should broaden itself to include the concept of an Indian Ocean Rim for socio-economic co-operation and other peaceful endeavors. Recent changes in the international system demand that the countries of the Indian Ocean shall become a single platform."[14] Formally launched in 1997, at Mauritius, the IOR-ARC Charter begins by embracing the past: "Conscious of historical bonds created through millennia among peoples of the Indian Ocean and with a sense of recovery of history; . . ." and then proceeds to lay out a vision based on multilateral economic cooperation.[15] From an initial membership of six nations in 1997 today it includes nineteen countries whose borders are washed by the waters of the Indian Ocean, but it does not include the Comoros, Somalia, Eritrea, Sudan, Egypt, Saudi Arabia, Qatar, Bahrain, Kuwait, Iraq, Pakistan, or Myanmar, quite apart from those that border the South China Sea. Whatever its limitations, the IOR-ARC provides a regional basis for beginning to build cooperative, multilateral regional strategies to address the most pressing problems facing the Indian Ocean world.

Considering the millennia of Indian Ocean history, how do its people and their governments remember their connected pasts? To take the last first, after decades of preoccupation with postcolonial nation-building, different governments have established museums and erected monuments to memorialize the past. Some of these have distinct nationalist claims, while others represent reconstructions of various ways in which a certain place is connected to the larger world of the Indian Ocean. The audiences for such official efforts are both domestic, intended to raise public consciousness, and global, intended to attract international tourists. There are too many of these to be listed, but among them is the Beit al-Ajaib or House of Wonders museum in Stone Town Zanzibar, where the interested visitor can examine a full-size mtepe that a master craftsman from Lamu built in 2003. Among the many cultural structures currently planned in the UAE is a museum dedicated to pearling and another to the dhow; a museum of slavery with an Indian Ocean focus is being developed in Qatar. The Western Australian Museum-Fremantle is an important center for research and exhibitions, while there is also a permanent Indian Ocean exhibition in the Western Australian Museum in Perth. An interesting new museum is the Aceh Tsunami Museum, opened in Banda Aceh in 2009.

The 600th anniversary of the first voyage of the Ming treasure fleets has generated more than a handful of Admiral Zheng He memory sites around the eastern reaches of the Indian Ocean world. Even though his body was buried at sea off the coast of western India, there are statues or museum exhibitions in Nanjing, Changle City, and Quanzhou in China; in Singapore, Melaka, Sarawak, and Java. These monuments signal recognition of the remarkable achievements of the fifteenth-century Chinese seaman by both China and the Chinese diaspora, but they also reflect the ambitions of a new outward-looking China.

Diasporas, the scattering of people from their homeland, have also generated important sites of public memory in Mauritius, where the Aaparavasi Ghat, commemorating the landing site for Indian indentured laborers in Port Louis, and Le Morne Brabant, a granite outcropping that was a refuge for runaway slaves on the southeast coast of the island, have both gained recognition as World Heritage sites from UNESCO. Many other national museums around the Indian Ocean have from time to time mounted exhibitions dedicated to various immigrant groups, such as that dedicated to Asian Africans at the National Museum of Kenya in Nairobi or one featuring art of the Chinese diaspora at the Ayala Museum in Makati City in the Philippines.

Diasporas have also generated various memories of homelands that have been expressed in both popular and literary culture. Here again there are many such examples, but a few from Mauritius will suffice. Not surprisingly, since there was no indigenous population at Mauritius, memory of where its people came from is a powerful element of their history, one that is intimately connected to Indian Ocean passages. The migration of Chinese workers to Mauritius is memorialized in Joseph Tsang Mang Kin's *The Hakka Epic*, first published in French in 1992. In this epic poem the writer both glorifies Hakka origins and lays out the poverty that drove them overseas in search of a better life. He also recalls the perils of oceanic travel in the line "No one wanted to face the Southern Seas." Later he writes,

Nobody thought of going overseas.
Nobody dreamt of trusting the wild seas.

Yet, he continues,

The seas saved us by hundreds of thousands.
The seas restored all our dreams and legends.[16]

A more immediate and painful recollection of an Indian Ocean passage is captured in a *sega*, the popular musical form developed by enslaved Afro-Malagasies and their descendants that has become a kind of Mauritian national music, sung by Chagossian Rita Bancoult.

My father, you're yelling "Attention passengers! Embark passengers!"
This madame, her husband's going but she's staying.

Crying, madame, enough crying madame.
On the beach, you're crying so much,
The tears from your eyes are drowning the passenger list.

Crying, madame, even if you cry on the beach, even if you cry
   Captain L'Anglois isn't going to turn the boat around to come
   get you.[17]

Song and dance figure significantly as vehicles of historical memory among all overseas communities of the descendants of enslaved Africans in both the Atlantic and Indian Ocean worlds. Not all songs are, however, so immediately associated with the sea or with the overseas passage as is this sad recollection of Rita's home on tiny Corner Island of the Peros Banhos archipelago that is part of the Chagos Islands, more than 1,000 miles from Mauritius.

A quite different example of how popular memory of origins is represented is the fascinating map of the Hadrami Indian Ocean network as seen from Indonesia. Published in about 2003 in the newsletter of the Hadrami genealogical organization Naqobatul Asyrof al-Kubro in Jakarta, the map has explanatory texts in both Arabic and Bahasa Indonesia that delineate Hadrami connections linking communities in Southeast Asia, India, Pakistan, Arabia, and Eritrea.

Memory of place is also embedded in modern literature. In the novel *Bénarès* by Mauritian author Barlen Pyamootoo, the narrator asks plaintively about the name of his village in the far south of Mauritius, "How would it make you feel to live somewhere and know there was somewhere with the same name in a different country?"[18] Although the name of this small village that was established around a sugar mill in Mauritius named Benares clearly derives from the colonial name for the Hindu holy city (today Varanasi) on the banks of the Ganges River, how it came to receive this name remains uncertain in the novel. What it does suggest is that for the millions of Indian Ocean people who were moved by force or by poverty to the far corners of this watery world their individual and collective memories are still powerful witnesses to the past.

While each of these examples demonstrate different levels of attachment to original homelands, the Indian Ocean also remains a region of cultural exchange. An illustrative modern example of this kind of cultural openness and flexibility is the story of the late Mzee Mombasa Mwambao, a well-known musician and comedic actor who performed for many years on both Kenyan radio and television. Mzee Mombasa was born in 1922 and raised in the major Indian Ocean port of Mombasa, from which he took his stage name. As a young man he shipped out on a dhow that carried mangrove poles, which were used for construction throughout the region, to the Somali coast. From Africa the ship then sailed on to India, where Mzee Mombasa spent six months exchanging musical ideas and learning about Indian culture. "We met a lot of good people in India, we had quite a few parties, mixing with the Indian women, and the Indian men, just socializing." He subsequently traveled in different merchant ships to South Africa, Somalia, the Comoros, and back to India, before returning to a similarly mobile life in East Africa. He recalls that "in all the places I visited we were treated very nicely because we were visitors and treated as guests."

Indeed, the concept of hospitality was an essential component of Indian Ocean world cultures. When he was in port, he seems to have spent much of his time meeting people; eventually he turned to music more seriously for his livelihood, becoming expert in performing Indian music. At one point he returned to India to record a play that he tells us "was a mix of Swahili and Indian," perhaps Hindi or Gujarati. Eventually, Mzee Mombasa settled down in Kenya, where he played the *oud*, a Middle Eastern stringed instrument that is similar to the Western guitar, in several different bands, including an Indian group in which he was the only African, before joining the Voice of Kenya in 1974 as part of their drama section. "So that's my little bit of history," he tells his interviewer, "I'm not sure if it is any good or not!"[19] In fact, Mzee Mombasa's story is a very good illustration of precisely the kind of mobile experience that lies at the center of Indian Ocean history.

The Indian Ocean world that has evolved over seven thousand years is very different today than it was in 5000 BCE. The dramatic evolution of maritime technology, the emergence and expansion of several major world religions, numerous attempts to impose political domination, as well as the constant movement of people, goods, and ideas have incessantly worked to transform this vast world region. If the basic geography of the Indian Ocean has been relatively stable, the names associated with its places and peoples have regularly shifted. Yet there are many deep continuities in the Indian Ocean, most notably the monsoon winds that determine its seasons and the ocean currents that wash its shores. Nevertheless, the historic ways in which human societies have nurtured their specific cultures over time, what is often called "tradition," remain significant in this ever-changing world. Never an isolated world region, the Indian Ocean is today more than ever a major world crossroads.

Chronology

CA. 5000 BCE
Earliest evidence of navigation across northern Indian Ocean

CA. 2000 BCE
Food crop exchanges between Africa and Asia

331 BCE
Alexander the Great establishes Alexandria, Egypt

CA. 100 BCE
Hippalus "discovers" the monsoons

1ST CENTURY CE
Periplus of the Erythraen Sea

CA. 100 BCE–400 CE
Earliest Austronesian migrations to Madagascar

CA. 411 CE
Buddhist monk Făxiăn sails through Strait of Melaka

622 CE
Muhammad's *hijra* from Mecca to Madina

670–1025
Srivijaya dominant state of insular Southeast Asia

869–883 CE
Zanj Revolt

977 CE
Earthquake destroys Siraf

1330s–1340s
Ibn Battuta visits countries of Indian Ocean

1390s–1515
Melaka dominates maritime Southeast Asia trade

1405–1433
Ming "treasure ship" voyages of Zheng He

1498
Portuguese enter Indian Ocean waters

1511
Portuguese seize Melaka

1589
Portuguese defeat Ottoman fleet at Mombasa

1600
English East India Company established

1602
Dutch East Indies Company created

1605
Armenian merchants forcibly resettled at New Julfa, Persia

1656
Dutch settle Cape Town

1749
Busaidi dynasty comes to power in Oman

1757
British victory at Battle of Plassy

19TH CENTURY
Massive Chinese migration to Southeast Asia

1806–10
British capture Cape from Dutch, Île de France from French

19TH CENTURY
British antislavery campaign in Indian Ocean

1822
British occupy Singapore

1826–40
Omani ruler shifts capital from Masqat to Zanzibar Town

1820s
First steamships in Indian Ocean

LATE 1830s–1910
Indian indentured labor replaces slavery in
many British colonies

1843
British establish Hong Kong, open China to
free trade

1853
British impose peace treaty on Gulf states

**1817–1822, 1835–1837, 1858–1859,
1865–1869**
Cholera epidemics sweep across Indian Ocean

1869
Suez Canal opens

1883
Krakatau erupts

1908–1938
Discovery and first production of oil in Gulf
region

2004
Asian tsunami

Notes

CHAPTER 1

1. Alan Villiers, *Sons of Sinbad: An Account of Sailing with the Arabs in Their Dhows, in the Red Sea, around the Coasts of Arabia, and to Zanzibar and Tanganyika: Pearling in the Persian Gulf: and the Life of the Shipmakers, the Mariners and Merchants of Kuwait* (New York: Scribners, 1940), 26, 14.

2. Ibid., 4.

3. William M. Holden, *Dhow of the Monsoon: From Zanzibar to Oman in the Wake of Sindbad—A Memoir of a Man's Adventure in His Youth* (Baltimore: Publish America, 2005), 34.

4. Ronald Latham, trans. and ed., *The Travels of Marco Polo* (London: Penguin, 1958), 43.

5. G. R. Tibbetts, *Arab Navigation in the Indian Ocean before the Coming of the Portuguese* (London: Luzac and Company. For the Royal Asiatic Society of Great Britain and Ireland, 1971), 192, 195.

6. Landeg White, trans. and ed., *Luís Vaz de Camões—The Lusíads* (Oxford: Oxford University Press, 1997), 6, Canto One, Stanza 15.

7. Ibid., 12, Canto One, Stanza 45.

8. Holden, *Dhow of the Monsoon*, 148–49.

9. The first poem is quoted in Himanshu Prabha Ray, *The Archaeology of Seafaring in Ancient South Asia* (Cambridge: Cambridge University Press, 2003), 53; the second is translated by Vaidehi and is available online at http://sangampoemsinenglish.wordpress.com/bartering-in-sangam-tamil/.

10. Ahmed Sheikh Nabhany, *Sambo ya Kiwandeo: The Ship of Lamu Island*, ed. Gudrun Miehe and Thilo C. Schadenberg (Leiden: Afrika-Studiecentrum, ca. 1979), 9–10. The *daradaki* was a forked stick used to twist the fiber rope after it had been poked through a hole in the plank from inside the boat in construction; *ushumbi* means a makeshift sail.

CHAPTER 2

1. Lionel Casson, *The Periplus Maris Erythraei* (Princeton: Princeton University Press, 1989), 63 (§21).

2. James Henry Breasted, *Ancient Records of Egypt*, vol. 2: The Eighteenth Dynasty (Urbana: University of Illinois Press, 2001 [1906]), 117, §286–88.

3. *The Kârnâmag î Ardashir î Babagân ('Book of the Deeds of Ardashir son of Babag')*, trans. Darab Dastur Sanjana, 1896, chap. 4, line 8: http://www.avesta.org/pahlavi/karname.htm, brackets in original; the definition of "Bokt-Ardašīr" is from http://www.iranicaonline.org/articles/bokt-ardasir-mid.

4. Casson, *Periplus*, 77, 79 (§43–46).

5. *Pliny the Elder, The Natural History*, trans. John Bostock London (Taylor and Francis, 1855), 6.96, http://www.perseus.tufts.edu/hopper/text?doc=Perseus%3Atext%3A1999.02.0137%3Abook%3D6%3Achapter%3D26#note-link34.

6. Ibid., 12.42.

7. Quoted in Kenneth R. Hall, *A History of Early Southeast Asia: Maritime Trade and Societal Development, 100–1500* (Lanham, MD: Rowman and Littlefield, 2011), 59.

8. The phrase is quoted in Wang Gungwu, *The Nanhai Trade: Early Chinese Trade in the South Chinese Sea* (Singapore: Eastern Universities Press, 2003), 34 and n.32.

9. James Legge, *A Record of Buddhistic Kingdoms: Being an Account by the Chinese Monk Fa-Hien of his Travels in India and Ceylon (A.D. 399–414) in Search of the Buddhist Books of Discipline* (ebooks@adelaide, 2010 [1886]), http://ebooks.adelaide.edu.au/f/fa-hien/f151/, chap. 40.

CHAPTER 3

1. Quoted in George F. Hourani, *Arab Seafaring in the Indian Ocean in Ancient and Early Medieval Times*, revised and expanded by John Carswell (Princeton, NJ: Princeton University Press, 1995), 77.

2. Quoted in Wang Gungwu, *The Nanhai Trade: Early Chinese Trade in the South Chinese Sea* (Singapore: Eastern Universities Press, 2003), 94. All text in square brackets are Wang Gungwu's insertions.

3. Quoted in ibid., 95.

4. Quoted in ibid., 73.

5. Quoted in ibid., 75.

6. Quoted in ibid., 93.

7. Quoted in Kenneth R. Hall, *A History of Early Southeast Asia: Maritime Trade and Societal Development, 100–1500* (Lanham, MD: Rowman and Littlefield, 2011), 130.

8. Quoted in Tansen Sen, *Buddhism, Diplomacy, and Trade: The Realignment of Sino-Indian Relations, 600–1400* (Honolulu: Association for Asian Studies and University of Hawai'i Press, 2003), 221.

9. Quoted in Hall, *Early Southeast Asia*, 131.

10. Translation available at http://noblequran.com/translation/surah31.html.

11. Quoted in Abdul Sheriff, *Dhow Cultures of the Indian Ocean: Cosmopolitanism, Commerce and Islam* (New York: Columbia University Press, 2010), 157.

12. Quoted in ibid., 158.

13. *Ibn Battúta, Travels in Asia and Africa, 1325–1354*, ed. and trans. H. A. R. Gibb (London: Darf Publishers, 1983 [1929], 110–11.

14. Ibid., 111.

15. Ibid., 112–13.

16. Buzurg ibn Shahriyar Ram'Hormuzi, *The Book of the Wonders of India: Mainland, Sea and Islands*, ed. and trans. G. S. P. Freeman-Grenville (London: East-West Publications, 1981), 103.

17. Quoted in Roxani Eleni Margariti, *Aden and the Indian Ocean Trade: 150 Years in the Life of a Medieval Arabian Port* (Chapel Hill: University of North Carolina Press, 2007), 153–54.

18. Quoted in ibid., 157.

19. Quoted in Ranabir Chakravarti, "Nakhudas and Nauvittakas: Ship-Owning Merchants in the West Coast of India (c. AD 1000–1500)," *Journal of the Economic and Social History of the Orient*, 43, no. 1 (2000): 52.

20. Quoted in ibid., 53.

21. *Ibn Battúta*, 234.

22. Ibid., 237.

23. Quoted in Ranabir Chakravarti, "Rulers and Ports: Visakhapattanam and Motupalli in Early Medieval Andhra," in *Mariners, Merchants and Oceans: Studies in Maritime History*, ed. K. S. Mathew (New Delhi: Manohar, 1995), 67.

24. Quoted in Hall, *Early Southeast Asia*, 294.

25. Quoted in ibid., 301.

26. Ronald Latham, trans. and ed., *The Travels of Marco Polo* (London: Penguin, 1958), 237.

27. *Ibn Battúta*, 287–88.

28. Quoted in Louise Levathes, *When China Ruled the Seas: The Treasure Fleet of the Dragon Throne, 1405–1433* (New York: Oxford University Press, 1996), 141–42.

29. Quoted in ibid., 170.

30. Quoted in G. Rex Smith, "Ibn al-Mujāwir on Dhofar and Socotra," [1985] reprinted in Smith, *Studies in the Medieval History of the Yemen and South Arabia* (Aldershot: Variorum, 1997), 3: 86.

31. Latham, *Marco Polo*, 298.

32. *Ibn Battúta*, 229–30.

33. G. R. Tibbetts, *Arab Navigation in the Indian Ocean before the Coming of the Portuguese* (London: Luzac and Company Ltd., for the Royal Asiatic Society of Great Britain and Ireland, 1971), 202.

34. Quoted in Wang, *The Nanhai Trade*, 98.

35. *Ibn Battúta*, 276.

36. Quoted in Xu Ke, "Piracy, Seaborne Trade and the Rivalries of Foreign Sea Powers in East and Southeast Asia, 1511 to 1839: A Chinese Perspective," in *Piracy, Maritime Terrorism and Securing the Malacca Straits*, ed. Graham Gerard Ong-Webb (Leiden: International Institute for Asian Studies; Singapore: Institute of Southeast Asian Studies, 2006), 225.

37. Quoted in Edward L. Dreyer, *Zheng He: China and the Oceans in the Early Ming Dynasty, 1405–1433* (New York: Pearson/Longman, 2007), 55.

38. Quoted in Margariti, *Aden and the Indian Ocean Trade*, 1.

CHAPTER 4

1. "Modern History Sourcebook: Vasco da Gama: Round Africa to India, 1497–1498 CE," http://www.fordham.edu/halsall/mod/1497degama.asp, §11. From *The Library of Original Sources*, ed. Oliver J. Thatcher (Milwaukee: University Research Extension, 1907), 5: 26–40.

2. Ibid., §12, 35.

3. Ibid., §27.

4. Quoted in R. B. Serjeant, *The Portuguese Off the South Arabian Coast: Hadramī Chronicles* (Oxford: Clarendon Press, 1963), 43.

5. T. A. Chumovsky, *Três Roteiros Desconhecidos de Ahmed ibn-Mādjid O Piloto Árabe de Vasco da Gama* (Moscow: Academia de Ciências da U.R.S.S., 1957), 47–48 (author's translation). Cape Guardafui marks the northeasternmost headland of northeast Africa, opposite Socotra Island.

6. Quoted in Giancarlo Casale, *The Ottoman Age of Exploration* (New York: Oxford University Press, 2010), 112.

7. Quoted in ibid., 101.

8. Quoted in ibid., 128.

9. Quoted in ibid., 125.

10. Quoted in ibid., 158.

11. Quoted in R. J. Barendse, *The Arabian Seas: The Indian Ocean World of the Seventeenth Century* (Armonk, NY: M. E. Sharpe, 2002), 130.

12. Quoted in Nancy Um, *The Merchant Houses of Mocha: Trade and Architecture in an Indian Ocean Port* (Seattle: University of Washington Press, 2009), 101.

13. Quoted in Jennifer Wayne Cushman, *Fields from the Sea: Chinese Junk Trade with Siam during the Late Eighteenth and Early Nineteenth Centuries* (Ithaca, NY: Cornell University Southeast Asia Program, 1993), 131.

14. Quoted in Barendse, *The Arabian Seas*, 477.

15. Quoted in Serjeant, *The Portuguese Off the South Arabian Coast*, 124–25.

16. "A Journal or Account of William Daniel His Late Expedition or Undertaking to Go from London to Surrat," in *The Red Sea and Adjacent Countries at the Close of the Seventeenth Century as Described by Joseph Pitts, William Daniel, and Charles Jacques Poncet*, ed. William Foster (London: Hakluyt Society, 1949), 69.

17. Quoted in Barendse, *The Arabian Seas*, 165.

18. Quoted in Sanjay Subrahmanyam, "Persians, Pilgrims and Portuguese: The Travails of Masulipatnam Shipping in the Western Indian Ocean, 1590–1665," *Modern Asian Studies* 22, no. 3 (1988): 516.

19. Jean-Baptiste Tavernier, Baron of Aubonne, *Travels in India*, trans. V. Ball (London: Macmillan, 1889), 255.

20. Quoted in Lakshmi Subramanian, "Of Pirates and Potentates: Maritime Jurisdiction and the Construction of Piracy in the Indian Ocean," *UTS Review* 6, no. 2 (2000), 21.

21. Quoted in Sebouh David Aslanian, *From the Indian Ocean to the Mediterranean: The Global Trade Networks of Armenian Merchants from New Julfa* (Berkeley: University of California Press, 2011), 49.

22. Quoted in ibid., 51.

23. Quoted in ibid., 206.

24. Quoted in Anthony Reid, *Charting the Shape of Early Modern Southeast Asia* (Singapore: Institute of Southeast Asian Studies, 2000), 135.

25. Quoted in Kerry Ward, *Networks of Empire: Forced Migration in the Dutch East India Company* (Cambridge: Cambridge University Press, 2009), 206.

26. Both quotes in Patricia Risso, *Oman and Masqat, an Early Modern History* (New York: St. Martin's Press, 1986), 14.

27. "Anonymous: A History of Mombasa *c.*1824," in G. S. P. Freeman-Grenville, *The East African Coast: Select Documents from the First to the Earlier Nineteenth Century* (Oxford: Clarendon Press, 1962), 217.

CHAPTER 5

1. Quoted in Michael Pearson, *The Indian Ocean* (London: Routledge, 2003), 196.

2. Quoted in ibid., 214.

3. Quoted in James Francis Warren, *The Sulu Zone, 1768–1898: The Dynamics of External Trade, Slavery, and Ethnicity in the Transformation of a Southeast Asian Maritime State*, 2nd ed. (Singapore: NUS Press, 2007 [1981]), 164.

4. Quoted in Donald B. Freeman, *The Straits of Malacca: Gateway or Gauntlet?* (Montreal: McGill-Queen's University Press, 2003), 180.

5. Quoted in Xu Ke, "Piracy, Seaborne Trade and the Rivalries of Foreign Sea Powers in East and Southeast Asia, 1511 to 1839: A Chinese Perspective," in *Piracy, Maritime Terrorism and Securing the Malacca Straits*, ed. Graham Gerard Ong-Webb (Leiden: International Institute for Asian Studies; Singapore: Institute of Southeast Asian Studies, 2006), 230.

6. Quoted in Gerald S. Graham, *Great Britain in the Indian Ocean: A Study of Maritime Enterprise 1810–1850* (Oxford: Clarendon Press, 1967), 377.

7. Ibid., 329.

8. All three quoted in Warren, *The Sulu Zone*, Appendix Q, 297.

9. Quoted in Warren, *The Sulu Zone*, 241–42.

10. Quoted in Warren, "The Iranun and Balangingi Slaving Voyage: Middle Passages in the Sulu Zone," in *Many Middle Passages: Forced Migration and the Making of the Modern World*, ed. Emma Christopher, Cassandra Pybus, and Marcus Rediker (Berkeley: University of California Press, 2007), 60.

11. Quoted in ibid., 62.

12. Quoted in Graham, *Great Britain in the Indian Ocean*, 394–95.

13. The entire treaty is reproduced in Charles Rathbone Low, *History of the Indian Navy* (London: Richard Bentley and Son, 1877), 1: 364, who specifically draws attention to the significance of this Article on p. 365.

14. Quoted in Pearson, *The Indian Ocean*, 199.

15. Quoted in Sugata Bose, *A Hundred Horizons: The Indian Ocean in the Age of Global Empire* (Cambridge, MA: Harvard University Press, 2006), 37.

16. William Heude, *A Voyage Up the Persian Gulf, and a Journey Overland from India to England in 1817* . . . (London: Longman, Hurst, Rees, Orme, and Brown, 1819), 21.

17. Captain G. L. Sulivan, *Dhow Chasing in Zanzibar Waters and on the Eastern Coast of Africa: Narrative of Five Years' Experiences in the Suppression of the Slave Trade* (London: Dawsons of Pall Mall, 1967 [1873]), 112.

18. In A. C. Madan, trans. and ed., *Kiungani; or, Story and History from Central Africa. Written by Boys in the School of the Universities' Mission to Central Africa* (London: George Bell and Sons, 1887), 44.

19. Quoted in Edward A. Alpers, "The Story of Swema: Female Vulnerability in Nineteenth-Century East Africa," in Claire C. Robertson and Martin A. Klein, eds., *Women and Slavery in Africa* (Madison: University of Wisconsin Press, 1983), 212.

20. In Madan, *Kiungani*, 112.

21. Petro Kilekwa, *Slave Boy to Priest: The Autobiography of Padre Petro Kilekwa*, trans. from Chinyanja by K. H. Nixon Smith (London: Universities' Mission to Central Africa, 1937), 10.

22. British Library, India Office Records, Mss Eur/F126/17, Sir Lewis Pelly Journals, Sir Lewis Pelly Journals, "Memo: of a voyage on board a Dingee (Sindee Boat) undertaken in the year 1841, from Kurachee to Bombay."

23. Quoted in Thomas R. Metcalf, *Imperial Connections: India in the Indian Ocean Arena, 1860–1920* (Berkeley: University of California Press, 2007), 165.

24. Quoted in Gjisbert Oonk, *The Karimjee Jivanjee Family: Merchant Princes of East Africa 1800–2000* (Amsterdam: Pallas, 2009), 24.

25. M. G. Vassanji, *The Gunny Sack* (Oxford: Heinemann, 1989), 9.

26. Quoted in Marina Carter and James Ng Foong Kwong, *Forging the Rainbow: Labour Immigrants in British Mauritius* (Mauritius: Alfran, 1998), 32.

27. Quoted in ibid., 51.

28. Quoted in Carter, *Lakshmi's Legacy: The Testimonies of Indian Women in 19th Century Mauritius* (Rose-Hill, Mauritius: Éditions de l'Océan Indien, 1994), 51.

29. Quoted in Leonard Blussé, "Junks to Java: Chinese Shipping to the Nanyang in the Second Half of the Eighteenth Century," in *Chinese Circulations: Capital, Commodities, and Networks in Southeast Asia*, ed. Eric Tagliacozzo and Wen-Chin Chang (Durham, NC: Duke University Press, 2011), 221.

30. Quoted in Carl A. Trocki, "Singapore as a Nineteenth-Century Migration Node," in *Connecting Seas and Connected Ocean Rims: Indian, Atlantic, and Pacific Oceans and China Seas Migrations from the 1830s to the 1930s*, ed. Donna R. Gabaccia and Dirk Hoerder (Leiden: Brill, 2011), 206.

31. Quoted in Claudine Lombard-Salmon and Ta Trong Hiêp, "De Batavia à Saigon: Notes de voyages d'un marchand Chinois," *Archipel* 47 (1994): 163 and 169 (author's translation of the French from theirs of the Chinese text).

32. Quoted in Anne K. Bang, *Sufis and Scholars of the Sea: Family Networks in East Africa, 1860–1925* (London: Routledge Curzon, 2003), 24.

33. Abdallah Salih Farsy, *Baadhi ya Wanavyoni wa Kishafi wa Mashariki ya Afrika/The Shaf'i Ulama of East Africa, ca. 1830–1970*, trans. and ed. Randall L. Pouwels (Madison: University of Wisconsin African Studies Center, 1989), 150.

34. Quoted in Bang, *Sufis and Scholars*, 60.

35. Quoted in Nile Green, *Bombay Islam: The Religious Economy of the West Indian Ocean, 1840–1915* (Cambridge: Cambridge University Press, 2011), 110.

36. C. E. B. Russell, *General Rigby, Zanzibar and the Slave Trade* (London: George Allen & Unwin, 1935), 79, 337.

37. Richard Burton, *Zanzibar, City, Island and Coast* (London: Tinsley Brothers, 1872), 2: 345–46.

CHAPTER 6

1. Wallace Stegner, "Discovery! The Story of Aramco Then—Chapter 1: Contact," *Saudi Aramco World* 19, no. 1 (1968): 11–12, http://www.saudiaramcoworld.com.issue/196801/ discovery.the.story.of.aramco.then-chapter.1.contact.htm.

2. Stegner, "Discovery!—Chapter 5: The Pioneers," *Saudi Aramco World* 19, no. 5 (1968): 16–23, http://www.saudiaramcoworld.com.issue/196801/discovery.the.story.of.aramco .then-chapter.5.the.pioneers.htm.

3. Mark Twain, *Following the Equator, A Journey around the World* (1898), Project Gutenberg EBook #2895, http://www.gutenberg.org/files/2895/2895-h/2895-h.htm#ch62.

4. Quoted in Sir Reginald Coupland, *The Exploitation of East Africa, 1856–1890: The Slave Trade and the Scramble* (London: Faber and Faber, 1939), 56.

5. A. J. da Silva Costa, *Guia do Canal de Moçambique* (Lisboa: Imprensa Nacional, 1878), 11–12 (author's translation).

6. "The History of Kua, Juani Island, Mafia," in G. S. P. Freeman-Grenville, *The East African Coast: Select Documents from the First to the Earlier Nineteenth Century* (Oxford: Clarendon Press, 1962), 299.

7. Carolin Liss, "The Roots of Piracy in Southeast Asia," Nautilus Institute for Security and Sustainability, http://nautilus.org/apsnet/the-roots-of-piracy-in-southeast-asia/.

8. Michael G. Frodl and John M. Manoyan, "Somali Piracy Tactics Evolve; Threats Could Expand Globally," *National Defense, NDIA's Business and Technology Magazine*, April 2010, http://www.nationaldefensemagazine.org/archive/2010/April/Pages/SomaliPiracy TacticsEvolve.aspx.

9. Quoted in "Piracy in Somalia," http://en.wikipedia.org/wiki/Piracy_in_Somalia.

10. Mohamed Ahmed, "Somali Sea Gangs Lure Investors at Pirate Lair," Reuters US, December 1, 2009, http://www.reuters.com/article/idUSTRE5B01Z920091201.

11. Quoted in Neil Tweedie, "Britain Shamed as Exiles of the Chagos Islands Win the Right to Go Home," *The Telegraph*, May 6, 2006, http://www.telegraph.co.uk/news/uknews/4200066/ Britain-shamed-as-exiles-of-the-Chagos-Islands-win-the-right-to-go-home.html.

12. Quoted in David Vine, *Island of Shame: The Secret History of the U.S. Military Base on Diego Garcia* (Princeton, NJ: Princeton University Press, 2009), 195.

13. Michael Wesley, "Sea of Discontent Threatens More Than Asian Unity," *The Australian*, July 27, 2012, http://www.theaustralian.com.au/news/world/sea-of-disconmtent-threatens- more-than-asian-unity/story-e6frg6ux-1226436149216.

14. Quoted in http://www.iorarc.org/about-us/background.aspx.

15. The Charter is available as a pdf file at http://www.iorarc.org/basic-documents.aspx.

16. Joseph Tsang Mang Kin, *The Hakka Epic* (Port Louis: President's Fund for Creative Writing in English, 2003), 24, 91–92.

17. Recorded in Vine, *Island of Shame*, 37.

18. Quoted in Thangam Ravindranathan, "Politics and Poetics of the Namesake: Barlen Pyamootoo's *Bénarès*, Mauritius," in *India in Africa, Africa in India: Indian Ocean Cosmopolitanisms*, ed. John C. Hawley (Bloomington: Indiana University Press, 2008), 181.

19. "Mzee Mombasa's Story," *UTS Review: Cultural Studies and New Writing* 6, no. 2 (2000): 181–85. Mzee Mombasa was interviewed with the assistance of a translator by Stephen Muecke in Mombasa on October 9, 2000.

Further Reading

GENERAL HISTORIES

Barendse, R. J. *The Arabian Seas: The Indian Ocean World of the Seventeenth Century.* Armonk, NY: M. E. Sharpe, 2002.

Barendse, R. J. *Arabian Seas, 1700–1763.* 4 vols. Leiden: Brill, 2009.

Chaudhuri, K. N. *Trade and Civilisation in the Indian Ocean: An Economic History from the Rise of Islam to 1750.* Cambridge: Cambridge University Press, 1985.

McPherson, Kenneth. *The Indian Ocean: A History of People and the Sea.* New Delhi: Oxford University Press, 1993.

Pearson, Michael. *The Indian Ocean.* London: Routledge, 2003.

Risso, Patricia. *Merchants and Faith: Muslim Commerce and Culture in the Indian Ocean.* Boulder, CO: Westview, 1995.

Sheriff, Abdul. *Dhow Cultures of the Indian Ocean: Cosmopolitanism, Commerce, and Islam.* New York: Columbia University Press, 2010.

DOCUMENTS

Casson, Lionel, ed. *The Periplus Maris Erythraei.* Princeton: Princeton University Press, 1989.

ANCIENT PERIOD

Hall, Kenneth. *A History of Early Southeast Asia: Maritime Trade and Societal Development, 100–1500.* Lanham, MD: Rowman and Littlefield, 2011.

Ray, Himanshu Prabha. *The Winds of Change: Buddhism and the Maritime Links of South Asia.* New Delhi: Oxford University Press, 1994.

Sidebotham, Steven E. *Berenike and the Ancient Spice Route.* Berkeley: University of California Press, 2011.

Wang, Gungwu. *The Nanhai Trade: Early Chinese Trade in the South China Sea.* Singapore: Eastern Universities Press, 2003.

BECOMING AN ISLAMIC SEA

Dreyer, Edward L. *Zheng He: China and the Oceans in the Early Ming Dynasty, 1405–1433.* New York: Pearson/Longman, 2007.

Horton, Mark, and John Middleton. *The Swahili.* Oxford: Blackwell, 2000.

Hourani, George. *Arab Seafaring in the Indian Ocean in Ancient and Early Medieval Times.* Revised and expanded by John Carswell, 2nd ed. Princeton: Princeton University Press, 1995.

Levathes, Louise. *When China Ruled the Seas: The Treasure Fleet of the Dragon Throne, 1405–1433.* New York: Oxford University Press, 1996.

Margariti, Roxani Eleni. *Aden and the Indian Ocean Trade: 150 Years in the Life of a Medieval Arabian Port.* Chapel Hill: University of North Carolina Press, 2007.

Tibbetts, G. R. *Arab Navigation in the Indian Ocean before the Coming of the Portuguese.* London: Luzac and Company for the Royal Asiatic Society of Great Britain and Ireland, 1971.

EARLY MODERN PERIOD

Aslanian, Sebouh David. *From the Indian Ocean to the Mediterranean: The Global Trade Networks of Armenian Merchants from New Julfa*. Berkeley: University of California Press, 2011.

Casale, Giancarlo. *The Ottoman Age of Exploration*. New York: Oxford University Press, 2010.

Das Gupta, Ashin. *The World of the Indian Ocean Merchant, 1500–1800: Collected Essays of Ashin Das Gupta*. Compiled by Uma Das Gupta. New Delhi: Oxford University Press, 2001.

Das Gupta, Ashin, and M. N. Pearson, eds. *India and the Indian Ocean Trade, 1500–1800*. New Delhi: Oxford University Press, 1999.

Miran, Jonathan. "Space, Mobility, and Translocal Connections across the Red Sea Area since 1500." *Northeast African Studies* 12, no. 1 (2012): ix–xxvi.

Pearson, Michael N. *Port Cities and Intruders: The Swahili Coast, India, and Portugal in the Early Modern Era*. Baltimore: Johns Hopkins University Press, 1998.

Pearson, Michael N. *The World of the Indian Ocean, 1500–1800: Studies in Economic, Social, and Cultural History*. Aldershot, UK: Ashgate, 2005.

Reid, Anthony. *Southeast Asia in the Age of Commerce, 1450–1680*. Volume 2. New Haven: Yale University Press, 1993.

Subrahmanyam, Sanjay. *Portuguese Empire in Asia, 1500–1700: A Political and Economic History*. 2nd ed. Malden, MA: Wiley-Blackwell, 2012.

Um, Nancy. *The Merchant Houses of Mocha: Trade and Architecture in an Indian Ocean Port*. Seattle: University of Washington Press, 2009.

Ward, Kerry. *Networks of Empire: Forced Migration in the Dutch East India Company*. New York: Cambridge University Press, 2009.

THE LONG NINETEENTH CENTURY

Alpers, Edward A. *Ivory and Slaves in East Central Africa: Changing Patterns of Trade to the Later Nineteenth Century*. Berkeley: University of California Press, 1975.

Alpers, Edward A. *East Africa and the Indian Ocean*. Princeton: Markus Wiener, 2009.

Bhacker, M. Reda. *Trade and Empire in Masqat and Zanzibar: Roots of British Domination*. London: Routledge, 1992.

Clarence-Smith, William Gervase, ed. "The Economics of the Indian Ocean Slave Trade in the Nineteenth Century." Special Issue of *Slavery & Abolition* 9, no. 3 (1988): 1–222.

Goswami, Chhaya. *The Call of the Sea: Kachchhi Traders in Masqat and Zanzibar, c.1800–1880*. Hyderabad, India: Orient Black Swan, 2011.

Graham, Gerald S. *Great Britain in the Indian Ocean: A Study of Maritime Enterprise 1810–1850*. Oxford: Clarendon Press, 1967.

Green, Nile. *Bombay Islam: The Religious Economy of the Western Indian Ocean, 1840–1915*. New York: Cambridge University Press, 2011.

Larson, Pier Martin. *Ocean of Letters: Language and Creolization in an Indian Ocean Diaspora*. Cambridge, UK: Cambridge University Press, 2009.

Metcalf, Thomas R. *Imperial Connections: India in the Indian Ocean Arena, 1860–1920*. Berkeley: University of California Press, 2007.

Miran, Jonathan. *Red Sea Citizens: Cosmopolitan Society and Cultural Change in Massawa*. Bloomington: Indiana University Press, 2009.

Prestholdt, Jeremy. *Domesticating the World: African Consumerism and the Genealogies of Globalization*. Berkeley: University of California Press, 2008.

Sheriff, Abdul. *Slaves, Spices, and Ivory in Zanzibar: Integration of an East African Commercial Empire into the World Economy, 1770–1873*. Athens: Ohio University Press, 1987.

Warren, James Francis. *The Sulu Zone, 1768–1898: The Dynamics of External Trade, Slavery, and Ethnicity in the Transformation of a Southeast Asian Maritime State*. 2nd ed. Singapore: NUS Press, 2007.

THE LAST CENTURY

Bose, Sugata. *A Hundred Horizons: The Indian Ocean in the Age of Global Empire*. Cambridge, MA: Harvard University Press, 2006.

Gilbert, Erik. *Dhows and the Colonial Economy of Zanzibar, 1860–1970*. Athens: Ohio University Press; Nairobi: EAEP, 2004.

Oonk, Gijsbert. *The Karimjee Jivanjee Family, Merchant Princes of East Africa, 1800–2000*. Amsterdam: Pallas, 2009.

Websites

The African Diaspora in the Indian Ocean World
http://exhibitions.nypl.org/africansindianocean/index2.php
The website contains a series of essays, dozens of images, several maps, and clips from documentaries to illustrate the dimensions of the African diaspora in the countries of the Indian Ocean. Based on an exhibition at the Schomburg Center for Research in Black Culture, New York Public Library.

The Indian Ocean and Global Trade
www.saudiaramcoworld.com/issue/200504/default.htm
Saudi Aramco World, a glossy magazine published by the Saudi Arabian Oil Company, includes accessible stories about the history of the Indian Ocean. It includes many photographs, maps, a timeline, and a searchable index to all previous issues of the magazine.

The Indian Ocean in World History
www.indianoceanhistory.org
Organized by Sultan Qaboos Cultural Center, Oman. Provides instructional materials for teaching about this region in the context of world history, including maps and a video introduction of a dhow sailing upon Indian Ocean waters.

Indian Ocean Trade
www.oxfordbibliographies.com/browse?module_0=obo-9780199846733
A bibliography by Edward A. Alpers for Oxford Bibliographies Online,

African Studies. Includes dozens of source citations with short descriptions of the place of Africa in the trade of the Indian Ocean.

The Indian Ocean World Centre
http://indianoceanworldcentre.com/
Hosted at McGill University, Montréal, Québec, Canada, the site provides information on the research and teaching activities of this important center of Indian Ocean scholarship, as well as links to other digital sources.

The Sealinks Project
www.sealinksproject.com
Information on current research, publications, and presentations on early Indian Ocean history by members of the Sealinks Project at Oxford University, a large multidisciplinary project involving collaboration with individuals and institutions around the Indian Ocean and beyond. It studies the earliest maritime connections that linked and gradually transformed societies around the Indian Ocean. The project draws upon the methods of archaeology, genetics, linguistics, and paleoenvironmental studies to understand the first steps toward globalization in the Indian Ocean world, exploring the interplay between the cultural and biological factors that came to shape societies, species, and environments in the region.

Acknowledgments

This book is the product of many decades of study, writing, and testing of ideas. Like most scholars of the Indian Ocean, I began my career as a student of one geographical subregion of that vast world, in my case of eastern Africa. But from the very beginning my focus on the ivory trade and slavery drew me into the waters of the western Indian Ocean and to the shores of the Gulf, western India, and the islands of the southwest Indian Ocean. From the late 1990s I deepened my research on the forced dispersal of Africans into the countries that rim the western Indian Ocean and its islands. This interest caused me to read more deeply about the territories where Africans had been removed and where they still live today. Then, in 2005, I began to offer a lecture course at UCLA on the history of the Indian Ocean, and those lectures served as a starting point for this book. Thus committed, I read as widely and deeply as I could about the history of those societies that rim the eastern shores of the Indian Ocean so that I might achieve some semblance of balance in the coverage of my lectures.

Not surprisingly, I have incurred many debts, both personal and scholarly, in arriving at this point in my career. First I must thank the late Richard Gray, who guided my 1966 dissertation at the School of Oriental and African Studies, University of London, and who encouraged me to follow the evidence that drew me from east central Africa out into the Indian Ocean. Next I should thank the Council of Research of the Academic Senate, the International Institute, the James S. Coleman Center for African Studies, and the Office of the Chancellor at the University of California, Los Angeles, for research and conference support that enabled me to expand my sense of the greater Indian Ocean and to meet so many international scholars who study this vast region. The wonderful library resources at UCLA, including its Interlibrary Loan Service, enabled me to obtain the sources, both primary and secondary, that have made it possible to write this history. In particular I thank Ruby Bell-Gam, African studies bibliographer at the Charles E. Young Research Library, for her readiness to help me obtain books and articles whenever I made a specific request. Colleagues at UCLA who sustained me on this journey of discovery, whether by answering questions, pointing me to sources, discussing ideas, or providing me with a platform on which to present my work include Andrew Apter, Sebouh Aslanian, Judith Carney, Jacqueline DjeDje, Christopher Ehret, Andrea Goldman, Nile Green, Amy Catlin Jairazbhoy, Vinay Lal, Françoise Lionnet, Ghislaine Lydon, Michael Morony, Merrick Posnansky, Ali Jihad Racy, Geoffrey Robinson, Michael Salman, Sanjay Subrahmanyam, Richard Von Glahn, Willeke Wendrich, and William Worger. In particular, I must thank Allen F. Roberts for being my partner in a number of Indian Ocean initiatives at UCLA. Several of my graduate students have also made important contributions to my understanding of the Indian Ocean world: Matthew S. Hopper, Phoebe Musandu, Randall Pouwels, and Awet Tewelde Weldemichael. I also want to thank the undergraduate students who endured my lectures and exams through four iterations of History 101 between 2005 and 2013. Their enthusiasm and their questions encouraged me to try to improve my teaching of Indian Ocean history.

Beyond UCLA the network expands considerably. Most significantly I must thank Gwyn Campbell, whose interests overlap so much with my own. Gwyn's organization of an important series of conferences at Avignon, France, marked a new initiative in Indian Ocean Studies. Now his leadership of the Indian Ocean World Centre at McGill University has created an important international space for Indian Ocean scholars. Equally, I want to thank Abdul Sheriff, both for his role as organizer of several Zanzibar International Film Festival conferences that provided an important venue for serious exchange of research, and for his critical collegiality over many decades. Michael Pearson is another long-time friend and colleague whose sharp critiques and exemplary commitment to Indian Ocean studies I value greatly. I am also grateful to Amy Catlin Jairazbhoy, Himanshu Prabha Ray, and Vijayalakshmi Teelock, each of whom invited me to coedit books with them that address aspects of Indian Ocean history. One peculiarity of working on slavery and abolition in this part of the world is that one receives invitations from organizers of conferences with an Atlantic focus to present a comparative perspective from the Indian Ocean. For these opportunities I thank Ana Lucia Araujo, David Blight, Michael Gomez, Robert Harms, and Paul Lovejoy. Indian Ocean conferences organized by colleagues in Western Australia have provided an important opportunity to present research at Perth and Fremantle since the late 1980s. Kenneth McPherson and Frank Broeze—both sadly departed—and Peter Reeves were instrumental in the original International Congress of Indian Ocean Studies jamborees, while Cassandra Pybus and James Warren were central for recent gatherings. Other opportunities were made possible by conferences or seminars at the Australian National University, Canberra; the CNRDS, Moroni, Ngazidja; Duke University; Monash University, Melbourne, Australia; Rice University; Spelman College; the University of California, Berkeley and Irvine; the Université de Paris 1; and the University of Pennsylvania.

In addition to those individuals already named above, I want to thank the following colleagues and students whose scholarship, comments on my papers, friendship, and collegiality have made my experience so rewarding. To be honest, these individuals are too numerous to name, but I must single out Richard B. Allen, Philippe Beaujard, Lee V. Cassanelli, Abdin Chande, William Gervase Clarence-Smith, Timothy Denham, Jan-Georg Deutsch, Shihan da Silva Jayasuriya, Pier Larson, Pedro Machado, Roxani Eleni Margariti, Jonathan Miran, Jeremy Prestholdt, Haripriya Rangan, Anthony Reid, Patricia Risso, Hideaki Suzuki, Shawkat Toorawa, Megan Vaughan, Thomas Vernet, Iain Walker, Kerry Ward, and Nigel Worden.

At Oxford University Press I must express my gratitude to my editor, Nancy Toff, who has been both very supportive and most tolerant as I toiled at this book. Thanks, too, to her editorial assistants, Peter Worger and Gwen Gethner, and to senior production editor Gwen Colvin.

Finally, there is my family. My children, Joel and Leila; their spouses, Melissa Fahn and Adam Moore; and their children, Asa, Dimitri, and Jude. Above all, there is my partner of more than fifty years, my clearest critic and superb editor, Annie, whose perceptive reading helps to make my writing as clear as it can be.

I dedicate this book to my oldest brother, Paul J. Alpers. Paul did not live to see this book in print, but his own career as a superb scholar and teacher, albeit in a field quite different from my own, makes this the right moment to recognize his love and his life.

Pacific Palisades and The Sea Ranch
May–July 2013

NEW OXFORD WORLD HISTORY

 The
New
Oxford
World
History

The New Oxford World History provides a comprehensive, synthetic treatment of the "new world history" from chronological, thematic, and geographical perspectives, allowing readers to access the world's complex history from a variety of conceptual, narrative, and analytical viewpoints as it fits their interests.

Edward A. Alpers is research professor of history at the University of California, Los Angeles. He has also taught at the Universities of Dar es Salaam, Tanzania, and the Somali National University, Lafoole. Alpers has published widely on the history of East Africa and the Indian Ocean. His major publications include *Ivory and Slaves in East Central Africa*; *Walter Rodney: Revolutionary and Scholar*, coedited with Pierre-Michel Fontaine; *Africa and the West: A Documentary History from the Slave Trade to Independence*, with William H. Worger and Nancy Clark; *History, Memory and Identity*, coedited with Vijayalakshmi Teelock; *Sidis and Scholars: Essays on African Indians*, coedited with Amy Catlin-Jairazbhoy; *Slavery and Resistance in Africa and Asia*, coedited with Gwyn Campbell and Michael Salman; *Slave Routes and Oral Tradition in Southeastern Africa*, coedited with Benigna Zimba and Allen F. Isaacman; *Cross-Currents and Community Networks: The History of the Indian Ocean World*, coedited with Himanshu Prabha Ray; *East Africa and the Indian Ocean*. His current research focuses on slave trade and the dispersal of Africans in the Indian Ocean world.

Index

CPSIA information can be obtained at www.ICGtesting.com
Printed in the USA
BVOW06s0529020616

450416BV00008B/18/P